STARTS – Science, Technology and the Arts

The artistic voices that DG CONNECT silenced

Being

A recounting, in a semi-surrealist manner, of observations made of the actions taken by the technocratic organisation known as the European Commission's DG CONNECT which led to the 'worst practice' case study that is STARTS

STARTS – Science, Technology and the Arts

The artistic voices that DG CONNECT silenced

Being

A recounting, in a semi-surrealist manner, of observations made of the actions taken by the technocratic organisation known as the European Commission's DG CONNECT which led to the 'worst practice' case study that is STARTS

by

Paul T Kidd

Cheshire Henbury

First published in 2016 by Cheshire Henbury. Ebook edition published in 2016

Paperback version ISBN 978-1-901864-22-9

Ebook version ISBN 978-1-901864-23-6

British Library Cataloguing in Publication Data: A catalogue record for this book is available from the British Library.

Email – Use Email Contact: www.cheshirehenbury.com/emailcontact.html

Web site: www.cheshirehenbury.com/science-technology-and-the-arts

To Presidents of the European Commission (past and present); to European Commissioners (past and present); to European Commission Directors General (past and present); to Chief Scientific Advisors (and former ones); to Senior Advisors for Innovation; to European Commission officials; to technocrats; to Scientists, Technologists, Engineers and Mathematicians and their artists in residence; to opportunists; to all those people and organisations who want to engage with artists for reasons of *art wash*; to all budding and practising communicators, visualisers, creationists, and manipulators of public opinion; to all those who speak nonsense about the use of art in research, development and innovation. Welcome to this strange thing that you perhaps want to call the nexus of science, technology and the arts, but which is not a nexus.

*Dark is the forest, with many outlaws there to be found; man-
eating tigers too! And into the forest they walk, thinking:
"what can possibly happen to us?" So blindly they stumble
forward; it seems they labour under many delusions.*

*Then the day is drawing long. Shadows are creeping slowly
forwards, and the way ahead is less clear. Strange noises fill
the air, and bright light, a thing of memory becomes. Gloom
then slowly descends, and a mist silently fills the air. Yet still
they press onwards, such is the confidence born of that elitist
inheritance that is part of their decaying world, the odour of
which so abundantly fills their fragmented minds. Soon they
find that their money is taken, to be given, a little at least, to
poor and needy artists. Then the night falls, and the Robin
Hoods flea, for the time of the tigers is near.*

*And what fool walks into a forest infested with outlaws and
man-eating tigers, and expects to come out alive? 'Tis a
question that within the pages to come will be answered
through words most strange indeed!*

*The moment of encountering those tigers is here – they eat the
bones as well!*

PREFACE

That which now lies before you, the *unfamiliar* content that forms this unusual book, you can like or dislike; this is your choice so choose. Yet, who among you knows the theories upon which this book is made, the aesthetic that has shaped its form, or what progression it represents in a life spent dancing with words? What do you know of the milieu that has shaped this dance, of the decades spent observing people, of being on the inside while remaining outside, and of a life-long engagement with the practice of *knowing how to see*? And what do you know of what it represents in terms of a step towards that which will come next?

Gyorgy Kepes said, in the preface to his book *The New Landscape in Art and Science*: "… preparing the book served as a kind of laboratory experiment …" and "… the visual and verbal statements neither parallel one another in exact correspondence nor follow one another in a strict causal chain. They complement one another in an interwoven sequence." Here too this applies. And then you ask: where are the visual elements? The answer is: find them.

Time now to use your *imagination*, which will transport you to another place, where it is a warm summer's evening. You find yourself sitting in Shakespeare's Globe Theatre on the banks of the River Thames in London. The play is *The Tempest*. You hear words; it is Prospero speaking:

"Our revels now are ended. These our actors,

As I foretold you, were all spirits, and

Are melted into air, into thin air:

And like the baseless fabric of this vision,

The cloud-capp'd tow'rs, the gorgeous palaces,

The solemn temples, the great globe itself,

Yea, all which it inherit, shall dissolve,

And, like this insubstantial pageant faded,

Leave not a rack behind. We are such stuff

As dreams are made on; and our little life

Is rounded with a sleep."

For many, the above represents the highest level of achievement of the expressive. But why is there so much ambiguity? And is it just the expressive, or is it more? Can a process that is grounded in the expressive also simultaneously be in the cognitive? Have you any idea what I am saying?

You have probably just learned something and you have only read a few words! What is it that most likely you just learned? The answer is simple: that there is more to using art in research than you ever *imagined*.

It is a truth, now becoming clear, that some artists have fallen in love with science and technology. And some scientists and technologists have also fallen in love with art, and together with artists they form the mutual admiration societies of art-science and art-technology. And being like lovers, they are inclined to whisper sweet nothings in one another's ears. Then into this love affair, steps a third party, known by the name of DG CONNECT. Now there is a love triangle!

"The medium is the message" said Marshall McLuhan. He also said: "Our conventional response to all media, namely that it is how they are used that counts, is the numb stance of the technological idiot." So while others look at the outputs of STARTS and proceed to jump around in celebration, here examined are the media called STARTS, DG CONNECT, their artistic collaborators, and the love affairs called art-science and art-technology, along with their silent narratives.

We once more appeal to William Shakespeare, to provide some words for these *star-crossed* lovers; words that, one might say, are *words of knowing*:

> *"Let me not to the marriage of true minds*
> *Admit impediments. Love is not love*
> *Which alters when it alteration finds ..."*

Here in this book, you will find an alteration! Let us see then, in due time, what unfolds in this love affair.

So back now to the matter of the style of the book, which one can say, *has made the familiar seem strange*. There is the *expressive*, and there is the *cognitive*, and betwixt the two?

Here is a book that you could now read. Or not! The choice is yours. No? Then end here! But I go on.

Thus now do I turn mine eyes away from Brussels, for in eastern skies ancient stars do rise, and when in this direction I gazed, *diamonds in the rough* did, in hazy visions appear, seeking transforming hands to cut from natural form to make precious sparkling gems as if by strange magic appear.

Paul T Kidd PhD, CEng, FIMechE, FIET, SMIEEE
September 2016

Art, ICT and STARTS: Charming Snakes

Black snake oil …

The conceited black snake was worried for black snake oil was failing and black snakes and their industry were being questioned. People were rejecting black snake oil and discovering that better snake oil could be found elsewhere. Black snakes self evidently needed to become more *creative* so that black snake oil would be more innovative. By becoming more innovative, it was hoped, black snake oil could be embedded more gracefully into society, or, to put it another way – black snakes would be able to manipulate people into accepting black snake oil.

The black snake, predatory as ever, caught sight of the white snake and saw in it an opportunity to reacquire some credibility and relevance, these now being long lost. It then rose up slightly from its coiled position and looked at the unsuspecting white snake.

The white snake had been lying quietly, in its innocence and naivety, and noticed the attention that the devious black snake was paying to it.

"That black snake is interested in me," thought the white snake, and, feeling charmed, it too rose up and both then looked at each other, neither blinking, for neither could.

The black snake too, even with its sense of superiority, was charmed, and it said to itself, "the white snake is interested in me." Whereupon it said, "I thought perhaps that we might CONNECT black snake oil with white, and explore its innovative potential." It then moved its head to its left, rising a little higher as it did so.

"Oh fantastic," thought the poor white snake, who was now much charmed. "The black snake is interested in white snake oil." Whereupon it said, "oh yes, black and white snake oil must surely go together." Then the white snake moved its head to its right, raising its head slightly higher as it did so.

The evil black snake was now even more charmed, because the gullible white snake wanted to CONNECT, and it thought to itself, "I was right, the white snake does have something that can enhance the creativity of black snakes and improve black snake oil." And then it said to the lowly white snake, "we should CONNECT black and white snake oil for this would be new." Then it moved its head to its right, positioning it even higher in the process of doing so.

The white snake followed suit, and moved its head to its left and slightly higher, feeling now very charmed indeed, and thinking, "the black snake thinks that CONNECTING black and white snake oil is new, so it said, "indeed we should CONNECT black and white snake oil, for this surely would be something new."

The devious black snake was now feeling very proud and charmed beyond anything that it had experienced previously, and it said to itself, "ah, so CONNECTING black and white snake oil is new, just as I thought," so it said to the increasingly charmed white snake, as it, the black snake, moved its head to its left and even higher, "we should undertake a study to show that CONNECTING black and white snake oil is indeed innovative and worth doing to enhance the creativity of black snakes."

The white snake was now lost in its desire to please the black snake and it moved its head to its right and tried hard to raise its head up to the level of that of the black snake, but failed to do so. As it did this, it thought to itself, "oh, it wants to do a study that will show just how innovative CONNECTING black and white snake oil is and how it will enhance black snakes' creativity." So it said to the deluded black snake, "I am very charmed that you think that white snake oil is so worthy of your consideration, but obviously it's a study that only white snakes can do."

"Yes indeed, and so it shall be" said the black snake which was now feeling so charmed that its vainglorious character became so obvious, but also thinking to itself, "and just to be certain, I will oversee this so that we arrive where I want to be." It then shifted its head once more to its right and rose even higher.

The sad little white snake, feeling charmed to a degree never before experienced, did then look into the matter of CONNECTING black and white snake oil, and lo and behold it did indeed find new evidence of the efficacy of CONNECTING these two snake oils.

The white snake had faithfully followed every move made by the devious black snake. As the black snake had just moved its head to its right once more, the white one also moved its head, this time to its left, but it was not now able to reach the height of the black snake's head. And then the white snake said, "behold new evidence."

And the white snake was just thinking, "this is just what is needed …", when: the evil black snake had seen enough, and being charmed now in the extreme, it CONNECTED with the white snake by biting it, devouring it whole, digesting it, and then, feeling charmed within itself, it set about doing that which it had always done, only calling it something different, and produced:

Black snake oil …

Art, ICT and STARTS: DG CONNECT and ICT ART CONNECT

One day, now in the past, I spent a day in the European Parliament in connection with initiative called ICT ART CONNECT. There I discovered things that now lead me away from DG CONNECT towards … This you may in time come to know. But for the moment I recount some of the things that I observed, starting on that day back in November 2013, or was is 1913? Sometimes it is difficult to tell!

The day in the Parliament was organised around a morning session of keynote presentations, which was chaired by Amelia Andersdotter MEP, and which included an address from the renowned artist, Roy Ascott. As for the afternoon session, a key part of this was a roundtable discussion chaired by Robert Madelin, at that time, Director General of the European Commission's DG CONNECT (the agency responsible for the ICT Research programme in Horizon 2020). Also involved in the roundtable were three members of the European Parliament: Maria Da Graça Carvalho MEP; Amelia Andersdotter MEP; and Morten Løkkegaard MEP.

I wrote a report about the roundtable discussion, which sets the scene for the ICT ART CONNECT initiative and highlights some important issues. Here I will present some further reflections:

Art is becoming popular! What was once mostly seen as a cultural activity is now being repositioned as an economic one, as evidenced by the European Commission's Creative

Europe Programme, which is now focused on encouraging artists to professionalize themselves and to seek to use their creative talents in the world of business. And universities too are being urged to address the creative arts, with *The League of Research Intensive Universities* advocating that art should be given a more central role in strategy, since it offers multiple benefits that range from scientific insights and educational quality, through societal value, to economic profit. It is not therefore surprising that research funding bodies such as DG CONNECT should be taking an interest in the creative arts through its fledgling initiative known as ICT ART CONNECT.

In brief, the idea, is to connect the European ICT and Art communities to foster productive dialogues, engagement and collaborative work between them. The interest expressed by DG CONNECT is for art to: contribute towards *enhancing creativity and innovation* in society, technology, science, education, and business; and *to help to more gracefully embed science and technology in society.*

There is of course nothing new in using art to develop ICT. Artists are already involved with ICT in their artistic practices. And this involvement turns out to be more than just using what is available, but also extending that which exists, as well as developing new ICTs. Additionally one can trace the involvement of artists in ICT back in time to the 1950s and 1960s, and Roy Ascott is one of the notable pioneers. Here also one has an example that goes beyond the notion of artist and technologist collaborating, to one where the artist becomes also the technologist to some degree. So evidently the use of art in ICT is more complex that it might first seem!

This then, in brief, is the background and more astute observers will realise from the above, that the involvement of artists in ICT research and development raises many complex issues and challenges, and that, with the tremendous potential, comes the reality that is very easy to create an unsuccessful initiative (not that anyone would ever admit to such).

One of the main concerns is that ICT ART CONNECT is just another example of government and economic interests appropriating art for their own agendas, which in this case, is the perpetuation of technocentric world views and progress defined in terms of increasing technological sophistication and materialism. And the words used by DG CONNECT certainty point towards this being their aim. And it can be noted that when DG CONNECT say that art can be used to contribute towards enhancing creativity and innovation in society, technology, science, education, and business, there is no self-reference to DG CONNECT themselves! Among the list of organisation in need of more creativity and imagination, DG CONNECT is most certainly positioned at the top of the list.

DG CONNECT speak of enhancing creativity in the ICT sector, but this raises the question of what exactly is wrong with the ICT sector (and others), if anything, that requires the appropriation of the artist's creativity? Yet to explore such a question is to admit that there might be something fundamentally wrong with the whole basis of modern science, technology and engineering. And this is something most definitely to be avoided, and hence one comes to this point: ICT ART CONNECT could become a means for those whom subscribe to technocentricism to avoid confronting the failing nature of this particular institution, thus providing the means of constructing a narrative that involves, in effective, making minor adjustments through a process of co-creation with artists (rather than implementing an artist-led research programme that is a direct challenge to the prevailing order).

The true value of art, which lies in allowing people to see the world in different ways and to envision different futures, is then lost because those with power, which is derived from money, do not wish the see the world in different ways or to envision different futures. And in this scenario, the artist once again has to become subversive, by simultaneously providing the much desired creativity while also, through their creative acts, demonstrating the true nature of what is happening.

Thus it can also be said that, yet another opportunity for Europe will be lost, simply because Prometheus, who, being bound to the rock of the past, is too busy reinventing himself in exactly the same form as he was yesterday, to be able to comprehend that he is doing this.

In such circumstances it takes an extraordinary set of events to set Prometheus free. In the Prometheus story this extraordinary event was Zeus allowing Hercules to break the unbreakable chains that bound Prometheus to his rock. In my novel *Moments in Time*, the central character is also like

Prometheus, and the extraordinary event that sets him free is essentially a ... If a told you it would spoil the story, and it is in any case something that is not for the telling, but for each person to find for themselves.

Art, ICT and STARTS: DG CONNECT – Out of time

At the START of 2016, the news was that DG CONNECT had just left the 1980s thanks to the efforts of the (now former) Director General, Robert Madelin. And as they begin the 1990s, the question remains: when will they enter the second decade of the twenty-first century, and experience 2016? The answer is, around about 20 to 25 years from now, so that will be about 2045 to 2050, by which time, China and India will have eclipsed Europe and most likely all its offspring as well, and the world will no longer be European, except of course Europe, for it has been condemned by Zeus and cursed by Nemesis, and DG CONNECT is the iconic representation of this.

DG CONNECT is an organisation that is out of time in every sense of the meaning of the phrase. They are not alone, also out of time are: Anne Glover (the former Chief Scientific Advisor to a former President of the European Commission); Richard Dawkins; Western capitalism; research, development and innovation practices, technocracy, ... Many things are now out of time, so many, that most actions undertaken today are flawed ones that will lead ultimately to disaster for humanity. Yet Prometheus sits on his rock and endures his agony for he can find no way to escape.

There is something that you need to know – your Age of Enlightenment science and technology is finished. It has run its course, and now the world is about to move on, leaving the European/Western world sitting on its rock. Good luck!

To be or not to be that is the question ...

Farewell DG CONNECT! Farewell Prometheus! Farewell Narcissus! We leave you with your self-inflicted art-science muddle: your obsession with art objects; your liking for performances; and your romantic delusions of working with the individual creative genius called the artist.

Art, ICT and STARTS: It is time for art

An input that I made to the consultation on the European Commission's FET Proactive Programme:

A long time ago, the word *science* did not mean what is does today and there were not the many and sharp disciplinary distinctions of the type that now abound in the modern world, which is a very *Enlightened* place – they believe!

The development of different disciplines has been explained by sociologists. It seems though that what they have to say is of no interest to those who engage in constantly referring to C P Snow's *two cultures nonsense*, and those who believe in the *da Vinci myth*. Both are interesting, but not for the reasons commonly associated with these two. Much of the art-science and art-technology love affairs are however erroneously justified by reference to Snow and da Vinci. Some people even say that art and science were at some stage in the past, united! Really, or is this another modern day urban myth: a case of people seeking to understand the past based on the present? A common mistake and one which is notably found in some work in the field of experimental archaeology.

Do we need to people who are polymaths, if there ever was such a thing? Or do we need people who can operate in the spaces between disciplines? While there will always be scope for the specialist, the person who, one can say, knows a lot about very little, such minds can be very dangerous. This applies to artists too, for in their world you will also find people with limited horizons, who are caught-up in the ideology of science and technology, and inclined to say very conventional things!

If we are truly to pursue the notion of sustainability we need minds that are not caught-up in ideologies, be they STEM, or art, or, a hybridisation (terrible word). We surely need people able to embrace more than just atoms, or cells, or whatever pretty pebble has caught the attention of a particular mind? Art too can be a pretty pebble!

Some artists say they are already exploring and researching the world from a transdisciplinary perspective, in which they bring art, science, and technology together in ways different from that of scientists or technologists, who most often limit themselves to narrow specialisations. And with this transdisciplinary approach, artists may well be demonstrating their potential capabilities to produce new insights and knowledge as well as new technologies. Whether this is the case, of course, needs much closer scrutiny. What do words such as multidisciplinary, crossdisciplinary, interdisciplinary, and transdisciplinary actually mean? It seems that they are often used – misused?

Many people however, especially those caught-up in specialisations, and those who think in terms of dualities, do not understand the potential of art in this transdiciplinary context. It seems that many scientists and technologists, who do encounter art in the context of science and technology, think that it is about illustrating their work and communicating this to the public. This is the nature of one of the gulfs that now exist, which is inhibiting the development of entirely new approaches to research, of several kinds, not just science and technology. Artists themselves however are also *muddying the water* and, in some cases, promoting the *illustration and communication* perspective. Another problem is that one is never sure if what is being said is a polemic, or just a gross over-selling of what they, artists, are actually doing. This is similar to those from the world of STEM who engage in *hype*! Perhaps *spin* is a better word?

Nevertheless there is tremendous transformational potential in art used for research, and this is fully in line with what FET aims at achieving, and to understand more about this I have provided an example of the creative arts used for research in the *Time for Time* consultation, which appears on my web site (See Appendix: web link #1).

Now I will add some additional points (which were not part of the original input): there are those who think that deploying art in research is about appropriating the artist's creativity in research activities leading to enhanced creativity and innovation. This is a manifestation of the *Ideology of Creativity*. This is foolish, yet it seems that such folly can be found in the European Commission's DG CONNECT. These are surely deficit thinkers; it is somewhat simple minded to reduce all Europe's problems to a lack of … Fill in the space yourself, according to your favourite deficit.

This tells us something very important about the nature of being human, of being European, regardless of whether one is living in a digital or non-digital era. Some aspects of being human, of being European never change, but it is about time that they were changed, before the madness that the European world is creating consumes everyone, regardless of where they live.

"Exploitation of artist is evil" was once said about Google's appropriation of art in their so-called DevArt. It is certainly time for art, but not through the appropriation of art by government agencies caught-up in technocracy, and technological determinism, which are pursuing familiar technocentric trajectories in support of neo-liberal agendas. Artists tempted to participate in such activities should reflect on these agencies as standing in the company of past appropriators of art – dictators, tyrants and popes. Food for thought for those tempted to follow the same route! You will be surprised by some of the comments that people from the world of STEM make, which exactly point to the need to take heed of this warning!

Art, ICT and STARTS: DG CONNECT classifies and symbolises technologists as the uncreative ones!

Following the ICT 2015 event in Lisbon, and the publication of the European Commission's new call for ICT research proposals, in the END, ICT ART CONNECT, or STARTS as it would now like to be known, appears in the new Horizon 2020 Work Programme 2016-2017 in the area of Information and Communication Technologies with a very traditional and very European approach, which STARTS with Classification and Symbolisation.

There are, we are told, two classes: technologists symbolised as the uncreative ones, who are suffering from a creativity deficit, which must therefore be corrected through collaboration with artists and creative people, symbolised as the carriers of the much sought after creativity (the weighty mystery). Yet what evidence is there for this creativity deficit? I look forward to reading the report that documents this evidence. I have searched for it using Google, but strangely, it does not seem to exist. Why could that be? Perhaps it is a secret report, only accessible to those with special positions, and not to be shared with invisible people such myself?

We are also told that arts are gaining prominence as a catalyst for an efficient conversion of S&T knowledge into innovative products, services, and processes. Again I searched on Google for the evidence of this. Truly there is a vast amount of information available about artists using S&T

knowledge to create art which is what artists do, but innovative products, services, and processes? I also looked for evidence of this in the ICT ART CONNECT study report. Nothing! And what a truly empty piece of work this is. It is one of those reports where there is so little content of value, material that would normally be relegated to appendices has been included in the main body of the report.

So I am mystified by this talk of efficient conversion of S&T knowledge into innovative products, services, and processes, and even more so when I read, for example, the Digital Humanities manifesto (See Appendix: web link #2), which clearly states that: "in the vast majority of cases, scholarship and art practice are not-for-profit endeavours whose actual costs far exceed real or potential returns." This corresponds with my own perspective and that of most of the artists I have encountered.

So it seems that artists are to be recruited to become the handmaiden's of the economy and of technologists, to create unconventional and compelling new products. Interesting opportunities here perhaps for some subversive activities to comment on the attitude of mind in government agencies, that, on the one hand does not prioritise or value artists, but which, on the other, seeks to appropriate them to the demands of an economic system that is failing and which has no place in a sustainable future.

"But there is eight million euros available" is your response. To which I would ask by way of reply: "just how

17

much of this will find its way into the pockets of independent artists?"

What is most likely to be the outcome of this exercise is that the bulk of the money will be placed in the hands of organisations. What individual artists will most likely receive, are the crumbs that fall from the table at which these organisations are dining at public expense. Be aware too, that the 50,000 euro experiments referred to in the text of the Call for proposals, is an upper value (the words used are typically below the range of 50,000 euro), and the amount is for the experiment, not for the artists. In other words, it will be shared among those participating in the experiments – artists and technologists, and perhaps others too.

You will not find in this new addition to the ICT Work Programme, any reference to the creation of art, which is what artists mostly want to do. And the STARTS prize seems, I must add, to be more about the European Commission in the form of DG CONNECT, seeking to acquire kudos from the arts – *art wash*. There is also no mention of artistic criteria in the selection of the experiments. And perhaps most noteworthy, no mention of using art to do all the important things that, at this moment, at this point in humanity's short story, are most necessary if we as a species are to have a future worth having.

Words one associates with art that are missing: aesthetics, artistic processes, art as a way of knowing the world, art practice as research, artistic freedom, imagination …

So what becomes of artistic freedom, when vainglorious technocrats in state institutions decree how art should be used and what subjects are legitimate? No need to answer the question for the answer lies in history, with Soviet Communism providing a modern example. And what to say about the notion of developing common work practices and identifying concrete Research and Development and Innovation problems that artistic practices could help address? Much, but this will do:

What is the point of the first, when the value lies in the approaches being very different, and for the second, well this is something that you should already know, if you understood and had taken the trouble to document the state-of-the-art and understand what art is about and how artists work. Which brings me to the sum of things: it was evident at the START that the European Commission did not understand; it was evident during the course of the development of ICT ART CONNECT that the European Commission did not understand and did not want to; and it is evident at the END that they still do not understand. STARTS, END, they are both the same, and an opportunity is once again lost. Never mind perhaps in 25 year's time the European Commission will take a fresh look, as they are doing with Social Sciences, to discover that which they have already been told, but have chosen to ignore. Only in 25 year's time it will be too late.

The realisation of ICT ART CONNECT in the new ICT Work Programme – a staggering lack of vision, imagination and creativity. Perhaps there is a creativity deficit after all, for here surely is the evidence. They should perhaps have practiced what they are preaching, and worked with artists to create an unconventional and compelling work programme!

ICT ART CONNECT DISCONNECT – the decision to disconnect and to hack ICT ART CONNECT is one of the most fruitful things that I have ever done. And the reasons for this will become clear over the coming years. ICT ART CONNECT, or STARTS, is about cognitive biases and deficit thinking, both being reinforced by artist who have fallen in love with science and technology who are seeking money. This is not the way forward for the arts.

So in the END you got what you wanted – money. Thus STARTS the rest of your life, without credibility and integrity. Enjoy the material rewards, for you have truly eaten of the fruit of the tree of knowledge.

And the END result will be an extremely noisy, highly schizophrenic circus, where all will be claimed to be a major success, but which will, in reality, be largely empty of substance, and once again the European Commission in the form of DG CONNECT will have demonstrated that it is truly a failing institution continuing to cause a huge amount of damage to the European economy.

Art, ICT and STARTS: Surrealists make of DG CONNECT the fools that they are!

Before me is a copy of the first Manifesto of Surrealism, published in 1924 and authored by André Breton, the writer who founded Surrealism. And what do I read?

"But in this day and age logical methods are applicable only to solving problems of secondary interest. The absolute rationalism that is still in vogue allows us to consider only facts relating to our experience. Logical ends, on the contrary, escape us. It is pointless to add that experience itself has found itself increasingly circumscribed. It paces back and forth in a cage from which it is more and more difficult to make it emerge. It too leans for support on what is most immediately expedient, and it is protected by the sentinels of common sense. Under the pretence of civilisation and progress, we have managed to banish from the mind everything that may rightly or wrongly be termed superstition, or fancy; forbidden is any search for truth which is not in conformance with accepted practices."

And this not only hints at the deep rooted cultural weaknesses of the Western (Europeanised) world, but well summarises too, DG CONNECT and much of what is (there are of course exceptions), the extremely noisy, highly schizophrenic circus that goes by several names: STARTS, STEAM, SEAD and probably several more as time moves on.

Oh *Vainglorious Enlightened Ones*, you weave narratives that speak of deficits, among which sits lack of creativity as one of many. Thus your fragmented and reductive minds, caught-up in strange notions of being rational and objective and basing decisions on so-called evidence (which seems mostly to be the means by which you reinforce your cognitive biases); construct your own reality made from the sum of simple problems befitting simple solutions; and then you do conspire among yourselves to appropriate art for the purpose of eliminating this one specific and imagined deficit, while arts' great figures of the past, make of you, the fools that you are, for unlike Breton, you have not yet even a glimpse of what the problems are and that you are but the manifestation of these problems, and that includes some artists too …

DG CONNECT had the power to choose and they chose wrongly. How does it feel knowing that by the time you do eventually understand, people who are not part of your Enlightened Europeanised world will have exploited your deep rooted cultural weaknesses and it will be too late? It has already happened once before, yet who among you know of this?

Oh dear! And I am only just getting warmed-up, for there are many more things to say about DG CONNECT, and its instrumentalisation of artists.

Art, ICT and STARTS: DG CONNECT and the tale of the Director General's new clothes

Once upon a time …

In the Emperor's Court, the EC, there was once a Director General (who I shall call DG) who met an alchemist. This alchemist whispered in DG's ear and told him of a magic way of making all those who research and develop Information and Communication Technologies (ICT) more creative and innovative. DG, being under political pressure to deliver innovation, was of course interested, for people were saying that innovation was sorely lacking in his particular area – at least that was how it seemed to the court followers who gathered around the EC. And being inclined, like many in the European world, the West, to think in terms of deficits, a simple self-constructed reality, DG was more than glad to think about a creativity deficit, and how alchemy possessed the power to correct this.

The alchemist also told DG that alchemy also possessed a special feature, that only those wise and clever would be able understand that alchemy has the power to cure the creativity deficit. Those people who did not understand this were fools and unfit for office.

And so it came to pass, that many alchemic events took place, and many people who were unable to understand how alchemy could cure the self-invented creativity deficit, kept quiet, for they did not want to be seen as fools or classified as being unfit to hold office. A special study was even commissioned which was full of new evidence of the creativity enhancing power of alchemy, yet none who read this report could see this evidence, but they kept quiet, for now also the smell of money was in the air – the special aroma of eight million euro. So, even more people were crying-out the message that the uncreative technologists needed the special creative powers of alchemists – turning lead into gold and all that stuff, or in this case, transforming technologists into creative people.

Thus it was that a new topic appeared in the Horizon 2020 Work Programme 2016-2017 in the area of Information and Communication Technologies – ICT-36b-2016: Boost synergies between alchemists and technologists.

Meanwhile, a little boy stood by watching and smiled to himself, knowing that those in the non-European world, in China, in India, and other places could learn from this sad but all too familiar tale, how not to approach the use of alchemy in ICT and other research areas. And thus armed, they would unleash against the *Vainglorious Enlightened Ones*, the forces of creative destruction, and these *Enlightened Ones*, not knowing what was happening to them, would retreat even further into the past, that place where they surely do belong.

Every sword needs a stone on which to sharpen it, so expect a lot more of these preliminary excursions into the fragmented stone-age minds of the *Vainglorious Enlightened Ones*, as bit-by-bit their strange and primitive beliefs, their rather odd ideologies and dogma, their silent narratives, are exposed to all those citizens that are, for very sound reasons, rejecting science and technology, and looking for something that the West (not even with all its STARTing, STEAMing and SEADing) will not be able to provide them with – life lived in balance and harmony and the science and technology that this will require. Here is a heresy on a scale beyond your worst nightmares …

"Great Scott! The man is surely mad, for he cannot see that science and technology are independent of culture, and must be the same throughout the universe."

"Leave Paul alone, you men with your patriarchal power structures, technological determinism and your positivism, expecting women to behave like you. Yes it's me, the crazy female artist known as Julia. Well, you wanted technologists to work with artists, so what exactly were you expecting? This is artistic freedom babe, and you don't like it, do you? And this reminds me, that I must put pen to paper and write about DG CONNECT, the Roman Catholic Church and the Soviet Communist Party."

Julia xxx

Art, ICT and STARTS: DG CONNECT and ICT-36b-2016: Boost synergies between alchemists and technologists

Specific Challenge: Innovation, today, is as much about the novel solutions that technology and design can provide, as it is about understanding needs of society and ensuring wide participation in the process of innovation. In this context, Alchemy is gaining prominence as a catalyst of an efficient conversion of S&T knowledge into innovative products, services, and processes.

The challenge is to accelerate and widen the exchange of skills of alchemists with entrepreneurs and technologists, thus creating a common language and understanding. This topic supports the STALCHEMY (S&T&ALCHEMY) initiative, fostering innovation at the nexus of 'Science, Technology and Alchemy'.

Scope: The activities are structured in two lines: establishing a structured dialogue between alchemists and technology developers and encouraging alchemists' integration into research and innovation projects, providing visibility of good practices and rewarding them.

a. Innovation Action establishing a structured dialogue between alchemists and technologists:

First, it will identify the relevant regional, national and international agencies active in education, research and economic support of the Alchemic Industries and:

- establish a Europe wide sustainable structured dialogue, ensuring the synchronisation of the efforts; as well as
- promote the replication of successful initiatives across other industries and European countries.

Second, it will directly support alchemists and technologists to work together and produce unconventional and compelling new products. Taking advantage of existing structures such as alchemy labs, creative and innovation hubs, the action should at least combine the following activities:

- Launch a yearly Europe wide competition for the best alchemist product ideas and ensure the financial support of their realisation. The action should cover the promotion of the competition, the selection process and support for the development of the selected ideas into fully functional alchemic prototypes. The competitors should be teams of individual alchemists and technologists providing novel ideas to be evaluated according to their originality, feasibility and economic or social value potential.

- Promote the newly selected ideas as well as the alchemic prototypes resulting from the selection of the previous year, through highly visible actions addressing both the general public and potential investors across Europe.

- Develop a sustainability strategy to ensure the persistence of the experiences gained and the coordination mechanisms set up during the action beyond the funding period.

b. Coordination and Support Actions

Proposals will cover one of the two areas defined below:

Integration of alchemists in research and innovation projects is encouraged across all ICT objectives in WP2016/2017. To facilitate this integration and help build silo-breaking partnerships between industries, entrepreneurs, and researchers in ICT with Alchemy, a Coordination and Support Action will provide a brokerage service that will:

- Fund short-term residencies/fellowships in running H2020 projects or in institutions and sponsor 'matchmaking events' (workshops, hackatons, etc.) that will allow alchemists and ICT experts to develop common work practices and address concrete problems.

- Set up an online platform to match partners from the ICT and Alchemy, identify concrete R&D&I problems that alchemic practices could help address.

- Organise an annual highly visible STALCHEMY event with international outreach bringing together H2020 projects, industrial players and alchemists and showcasing successful interactions between industry, technology and Alchemy.

Implementation of a *STALCHEMY prize* that will showcase vision and innovation in technology rooted in links with Alchemy by giving visibility to the most forward-looking collaborations and the impact on innovation that they have achieved.

Expected Impact:

- Provide the European landscape with sustainable structured dialogues between alchemists and technologists.
- Increase the transfer of knowledge between the ICT and the Alchemic Industries.
- Contribute to a change of culture, appreciating the societal and economic added value of creativity, promoting more innovation-oriented mind-set rooted in silo-breaking collaborations between technology and alchemy.

Acknowledgement: The above is based on the text of the ICT Work Programme 2016-2017. Thanks to the European Commission's DG CONNECT for providing content that was so easy to parody!

Alchemy! Well, why not? Isaac Newton was a practicing alchemist so it must be a good idea. He was also a theologian as well. A very early example of one of the

Enlightened Ones crossing disciplinary boundaries – operating at the nexus of natural philosophy and alchemy, the nexus of natural philosophy and religion. Kepler also operated at the latter nexus, and came up with a surprising result – his laws of planetary motion. Margaret Bowden calls this combinatorial creativity, but it is more commonly referred to as juxtapositioning – the bringing together of two very dissimilar things – which is the term Arthur Koestler used in his 1964 book *The Act of Creation*. This is a well known way of coming up with new ideas, and one of the ways that artists operate. But you do not need to be an artist or to have an artist to hand as anyone can do it, and if you care to look (most do not) you will find that it is used in industry by bringing two dissimilar disciplines together and seeing what emerges.

Being crazy is obviously a good thing! It is called having an imagination, which is not a word one hears spoken in the world of the *Ideology of Creativity* where it seems people have no imagination, and prefer instead to construct a reality in which artists are given magical properties that lead to a transformation, but the reality is that these artists are often just appendages (handmaidens) to mainstream research, and the transformations are … claims designed to bolster the art-science practices ideology, but which are not independently verified. So, second order cybernetics comes into play! This is also a recipe for creating a highly discredited zone of practice which will do irreparable damage to the notion of the artist as researcher and practice-led and practice-based research.

We need a professional and highly innovative approach to the challenge of bringing artists into research and development processes and this involves using art in an imaginative way! Self-evidently this was too much to expect from DG CONNECT.

Art, ICT and STARTS: DG CONNECT and "I'm out of my comfort zone"

"I'm out of my comfort zone."

So said Robert Madelin, (at the time) Director General of DG CONNECT, on November 11th 2013, while chairing an ICT ART CONNECT workshop, hosted in the European Parliament buildings.

"Oh Robert dear, out of your comfort zone indeed! You and your people were also way out of your depth as well, but you would not think so by the way those you assigned to develop ICT ART CONNECT behaved.

"Yes it's me, Julia, feminist artist, and the creative part of the schizophrenic artist-technologist pairing known as Julia and Paul, or as Paul likes to say, Paul and Julia. Paul is the technologist, the uncreative one, who is suffering from a creativity deficit!

"You've moved on so are no longer responsible for DG CONNECT, but we watched and recorded the whole story of ICT ART CONNECT and archived all the material so that when some, not so far future art-history researcher, decides to research and write about another chapter in the already long story of art-technology and art-science, all the relevant material will be available. It's called open access! And the story continues and it seems almost weekly people are saying ridiculous things, and we continue to collect and archive this, so that history will not forget who said what and just how ridiculous they were.

"What's that Robert, you did not realise that you and your colleagues would become part of history. Too late now! It will make an interesting chapter: 'The Tale of the Director General's new clothes: The European Commission's appropriation of art to the *Ideology of Creativity.*'

"And now of course, the rest of the world, will know how not to go about involving artists in technological research and innovation. Your people should have listened to Paul, because he has long experience of unconventional transdisciplinary activity, and he told your colleagues that it did not matter what the European Commission thought, wanted, or decided, for what would be more important would be what China and India decided to do. You listened to the wrong people, yet again. You listened to those who shouted the loudest. You fell foul, once again, of those allegedly, morally corrupt relationship that the Commission often forms with experts – the ones hinted at by the former Chief Scientific Advisor to a former President of the European Commission – where the European Commission seeks the opinions of experts willing to go along with what the Commission has decided to do. And you did this because you have a political agenda that involves the instrumentalisation of art and artists.

"Never mind, as DG CONNECT begins to experience the 1990s, 25 five years from now, some future Director General, of some future successor Directorate General of DG CONNECT, might discover what ICT ART CONNECT should have done, but won't know that there was such a thing

33

as ICT ART CONNECT. This is what Paul has come to call the 20-25 year rule: The European Commission eventually does the right thing only 20-25 years after it was relevant. SSH engagement is the classic example of this – first recommended by the FAST Programme in the early 1990s, and what did ESPRIT programme do in response? Nothing! It was recommended again in 2004 by an ISTAG working group and what did DG INFSO do? Nothing of note! And now, in the new work programme, DG CONNECT is, as the document states, *taking a fresh look* at that which others have looked at since the beginning of the 1980s. But you have not even taken a serious first look so how can you take a fresh look?

"Paul wrote something that is very relevant to this. I quote him here: 'Europe has become like Prometheus. Everyday Europe reinvents itself in exactly the same form that it was the day before, being as it is, bound, by invisible and silent chains, to the rock of the past, and unable to escape from it. And Europe has so fallen in love with itself that it is unable to see this. Thus will the past become the future! Europe has been condemned by Zeus and cursed by Nemesis. There is no Hercules to set Europe free. And using such knowledge, China and India can unleash against Europe the forces of creative destruction, and Europe will not understand what is happening, but will instead retreat even further into the past, for this is what civilisations that are in a state of collapse do. And the case of the former Chief Scientific

Advisor is a very good example of someone retreating into the past.'

"This is also the fate that awaits the proposed European Innovation Council!

"Art in technological research and innovation – it's not about bringing creativity to scientists, technologists, or engineers! They are already creative.

"And so you ask, what is it about?

"Too late now, you will just have to wonder about that, for Paul and I are not going to tell you, and it seems that most of the art people that the European Commission associates with are not going to tell you, or are not able to do so. But Paul and I will create a theory, so written that you will not understand it. And to those who can, the future belongs …"

Julia, xxx

Art, ICT and STARTS: DG CONNECT and "He's too theoretical"

Following on from the previous chapter, we now explore one of the reasons why we are not going to tell DG CONNECT anything, nor even explain what this means (surely you do not think that you understand the meaning of this?), and why we will make a theory of art-science and art-technology practices that DG CONNECT and the other *Vainglorious Enlightened Ones*, will struggle to understand. And part of the reason lies in this statement:

"He's too theoretical."

This staggeringly ignorant remark was made by a European Commission bureaucrat in DG CONNECT, about the British Artist Roy Ascott, following Ascott's stimulating, enlightening and inspirational presentation in the European Parliament on the morning of November 11, 2013, in the keynote speaker session that preceded the ICT ART CONNECT workshop that was chaired by Robert Madelin, at that time Director General of DG CONNECT.

"It's Julia again Robert. I just thought that you and the rest of the world should know the attitude that prevails in the minds of technocrats who do not know the limits of their own knowledge. People who would, rightly, think someone ridiculous if they were to suggest that a quantum computer could be researched and developed without using quantum theory, but condescendingly think that art can be brought into research, development and innovation processes without using art and literary theory, and other theories too. But care you? No you do not, for you are just using art and artists as an instrument to achieve political ends.

"It turns out that theory is everything, in more ways than one. Paul and I knew this, and we knew also that those caught-up in the dogma and ideology of Western science and technology would not accept this. Paul gave it a name – the Prometheus syndrome. And this is how the Chinese, the Indians, and others from the non-European world will give Europe and the rest of the West, the economic thrashing that they deserve. And Paul and I will help them for we are sorely tired of what we describe as the *Vainglorious Enlightened Ones* and their collective delusions and constructed realities and what they are doing to our world in the name of that stupid idea that they call progress – that's theory again.

"Theory is dead you say! Wishful thinking perhaps? Long live theory we say, for we are not caught-up in your very strange Western dualities and your very Abrahamic notions of sole truth and the one best way. A theory of everything, so to speak, which also includes the plainly ridiculous things that people often do and say, when, to this mysterious nexus, with their delusions, they do puzzlingly and momentarily gravitate.

"Come to know us in many different ways ..."

Julia, xxx.

Art, ICT and STARTS: DG CONNECT and yet another meeting of the STARTS circus in the European Parliament

Advertised in late 2015 was a meeting, to be staged in the European Parliament, of the highly schizophrenic, extremely noisy circus that is STARTS. This was the third time that such a meeting was hosted in the European Parliament buildings. Interesting!

A grand total of three European Commissioners have also now lent their support to ICT ART CONNECT and STARTS, but being politicians they will not know what they are talking about, as was the case when the former Chief Scientific Advisor to a former President of the European Commission turned up at an ICT ART CONNECT meeting talking nonsense about art and science. Interesting!

And we have this rather empty ICT ART CONNECT study report that contains some strange statements that, should you care to explore them further: under normal circumstances such a report would be an embarrassment to DG CONNECT, but it is not! Interesting!

As to the matter of the application of due diligence procedures before including STARTS in the new, 2016-17, ICT Workprogramme – none can be detected. Interesting!

It has become very evident that DG CONNECT is out of its depth, and they have once more engaged in their usual habit of forming those allegedly morally corrupt relationships with their experts. Interesting!

It can also be seen that various other people are jumping on the bandwagon – me too they cry, and in doing so are reinforcing a delusion! And I am sure that there are many more who will want to join in. Plenty of opportunities to say ridiculous things! Interesting!

And then there are the Members of the European Parliament who also want to lend their names to this circus. Interesting!

In a different place, people are talking about how they bring their artistic hobbies to work and have started making claims about new discoveries made because of this, but of note, is a lack of critical assessment of such claims. Positivism, is seems, flies away when it is found to be inconvenient. Interesting!

Elsewhere too, many people (mostly scientists, technologists, engineers and mathematicians) with vested interests, are talking, in a manner that mostly amounts to baby talk, about art-science and art-technology practices, yet seem not to be aware that their discussion are at such a level, or if they are, are not concerned about it. Interesting!

The growing interest in the so called nexus of art-science, or art-technology, is happening at a moment in time when people are beginning to understand just what scientists, technologists, engineers and mathematicians are doing to our world in their role as handmaidens to economic interests: global warming; acid rain; ozone depletion; desertification; mass extinction; lowering of river levels and water tables; bacteria resistance to anti-biotics; resource depletion;

Fukushima; plastics polluting the world's oceans; nitrate contamination of water resources; destruction of habitats; ... The list is too long to continue, but they are all brought to you courtesy of scientists, technologists, engineers and mathematicians (STEM people)! Interesting!

So what is going on? Why is art-science and art-technology being hyped-up, turned into the latest fad, and politicised? We know of course that the smell of money is in the air and that there is an opportunity for – 15 minutes of fame! And self-evidently people are now re-branding what they do (for example UX) and calling it by a new name (STARTS). But what does all this mean for the notion of a fair and proper evaluation of the proposal submitted to ICT Topic 36? Are the results already known to DG CONNECT?

I have seen these very noisy circuses before and they all end the same way, with little to show, for they are all style and little substance, and most of what goes on, is already what has been done under a different name. The result of STARTS will be that some people will have bigger bank balances, but the public will be out-of-pocket, with, most likely, nothing very much to show for the expenditure of their hard earned money. Collectively people seem determined to make of themselves fools, by declaring that the emperor is wearing a fine suite of clothes when in fact the emperor is naked. This perhaps is the nature of the Emperor's Court, the EC, otherwise known as the European Commission. STARTS is about style and has very little to do with substance, for what substance there is, already exists. It is about image making – DG CONNECT's image! Art wash!

It is now very clear that the European Commission are playing a political game, and are using art and artists for political reasons, so all those concerns about instrumentalisation turned out to be very well founded indeed.

"The grazing herd has arrived! It will of course eventually move on in search of fresh pastures, but that zone of discredited practice looms large because of all the dung that it will leave behind. Yet …

"I am wondering why this opportunity has presented itself to us. All this dung! Any thoughts about this Julia?"

"Yes Paul, indeed I have for we will use it to fertilise our thinking, so keep it coming, for all the nonsense, the emptiness, the re-branding, the grasping at straws, the vain attempts to find some justification for working with artists, feeds us, sharpens our minds, and, in the process of developing our critique, helps us to know in ways that seem to lie far beyond the very limited horizon of this grazing herd. While you are busy pulling at the meagre grass and chewing the cud, we fly as eagles and see as a result, a very different world that is most certainly not dirt and grass."

Art, ICT and STARTS: DG CONNECT and Being John Malkovich

So, the European Commission's ICT ART CONNECT initiative and the follow-on, the STARTS Platform! Quite a performance, but nothing at all compared with the one that I am STARTing ...

Being John Malkovich – I: In this surrealist comedy, a puppeteer takes a temporary job as a filing clerk. While at work, the puppeteer discovers a portal that leads into the mind of the renowned actor, performer, and artist known by the name of John Malkovich. The puppeteer then decides to enter the mind of John Malkovich to independently and objectively observe the life of John Malkovich, but being a puppeteer, ends up manipulating and using John Malkovich, thus changing John Malkovich to reflect the interests and objectives of the puppeteer.

Being John Malkovich – II: In this surrealist comedy, a civil servant, a puppeteer, takes a temporary job as head of a failing public sector organisation. While at work, the puppeteer discovers a portal that leads into the mind of renowned actor, performer, and artist known by the name of John Malkovich. The puppeteer then decides to enter the mind of John Malkovich to independently and objectively observe the life of John Malkovich, but being a puppeteer, ends up manipulating and using John Malkovich, thus changing John Malkovich to reflect the interests and objectives of the puppeteer.

Being John Malkovich – III: In this surrealist comedy, a cybernetician who knows that he is a puppeteer, just becomes the renowned actor, performer, and artist known by the name of John Malkovich. Being such, he then writes, stages, directs and performs in, something the likes of which has never been seen before, and in doing so, not only reveals that which is universal to all puppeteers, but shows the path towards a different way of knowing and doing based on an understanding of what it is to be puppeteer.

The instrumentalisation of DG CONNECT – they never expected that! The performance has only just begun!

Now you ask: why such a performance?

Art, ICT and STARTS: DG CONNECT and two European Commissioners in conversation with Julia

"Hi there all you artistic folk, it's me, Julia, part of that highly schizophrenic art-technology pairing known as Julia and Paul.

"Today I have with me two European Commissioners who will say something about this thing called the nexus of art and science.

"So Commissioner Moedas, what would you like to say about this topic?"

"Yes, thank you Julia. Let me first say that it is a great pleasure to be here with you today. I think that more and more we all understand that innovation in the future will be on the intersection of arts and sciences."

"Great. Now how did you come to such a conclusion?"

"Scriptwriter! Where's my scriptwriter?"

"Well Commissioner while you and your scriptwriter are being creative and trying to find an innovative answer to this simple question, we'll move on to Commissioner Oettinger. What would you like to contribute to this fascinating discussion?"

"I too would like to say that it is a great pleasure to be here with you today. Artistic creativity and critical thinking are essential for innovation in today's digital world. Already, highly innovative companies like Mercedes thrive on a strong link between artists and their engineers. The EU will support [such] multidisciplinary themes in H2020."

"Well said Commissioner. Did you know that in the medieval and the renaissance periods the Roman Catholic Church also thrived on a strong link with artists. The Communist State in the Soviet Union also thrived on the very strong and rigid links that it forged with artists. So clearly, thriving on strong links with artists can mean many things. It seems that the European Commission is also forging strong links with artists too! Are they also rigid as well? But while you are pondering on these questions, I'm glad you mentioned Mercedes, because we just happen to have here a representative from Mercedes Finance in the United States. Please tell us something about the strong links you have forged with the art world."

"Indeed Julia I would be very glad to do so. We work with an art gallery where our employees view masterpieces by artists such as Diego Rivera, Rembrandt and Picasso. A trained facilitator then asks for their impressions during post-viewing meetings. During the debriefing session, we touch on how art applies to business and think about how employees can make use of more creativity at work and offer different solutions to our customers. Participants engage in collaborative discussion and offer answers to messages suggested by the art they view. However, to ask employees to completely connect the art experience to their jobs is forcing it too far. Nevertheless, a business-art relationship offers many advantages. It's about cognitive diversity. The way people think is based on where they come from. Art reflects the diversity of the world, the workplace and the people in it."

"So, looks much as though this is just a more sophisticated form of corporate sponsorship of the arts, primarily designed for the purposes of image making – your image! If it is the case that your employees are not sufficiently creative at work, were there no thoughts in your mind that there might be problems with your internal organisational design, or with the company culture, or with employee tasks and roles, or the way they are treated and rewarded, or with the attitude that prevails among middle and senior management? Or are you in need of a visit to the art gallery before you are able to have such thoughts?

"So there you have it – employees with a creativity deficit! The *Ideology of Creativity* – founded on an imaginary deficit.

"And I see that the European Commissioners and the Mercedes' representative have left us. No doubt to reflect upon what they have learned here today. Or perhaps not! They are after all puppeteers ... And men!

"Coming soon – more about the *Ideology of Creativity*. And I will be asking more questions about this company called Mercedes and exploring just what they have been doing with artists – more image making! Literally!

"This is Julia signing off, xxx."

Art, ICT and STARTS: DG CONNECT Theatre – the ICT 2015 Performance 'Driving Innovation through Creativity and the Arts'

The actors assemble on the stage, each knowing their lines, while those who will be their audience take their seats and wait expectantly for the start of the performance *Driving Innovation through Creativity and the Arts*. The odour of money drifts through the theatre with its stale recycled and specially conditioned air, intoxicating all who enter the room, inducing an insanity that only puppeteers acting collectively can bring into being, as once more they proceed to construct one of their many convenient realities. And watching in another time and place, are Julia and Paul, who have come to see if, by some quirk of serendipity, something of substance may transpire, but mainly it is their intention to observe the playing out of what has already become a tragedy of errors and a comedy of errors both at the same time.

On the stage also is the one who will direct this theatre, and then they START, as one by one each plays their part, which is to heavily pitch themselves and their organisations, and it seems, to out-do one another in the number of times they speak the very special and magical word that is *creativity*, which is soon worn out with use, but left very much unexamined, nor it seems understood, for what is taking place before Julia and Paul's eyes can in no way be described as the outcome of creative minds, except perhaps those found in marketing departments. And in noting all the emptiness, Julia

47

speaks to Paul with silent words, which Paul, reading her lips, quickly comes to understand, as "some are clearly speaking of UX design." Oh dear! The circus has indeed come to town, and consequently it will probably never be known if there is anything beyond this.

Julia now is pointing out, that Mercedes Man, has said virtually nothing, so to Google Paul does turn to seek out the results for Mercedes and this word *Ideation*, and lo and behold what does he find, but many pictures drawn by artists of future modernistic car designs, which, as Julia is now saying, is typical of men who to image making often turn when what is needed are the communication of that which might at least pass for words containing something of a more substantial form. And once again Mercedes are shown to be, literally, engaged in image making.

Looking now at a very futuristic automatic car, that on the web can also be found, she speaks again these words – "probably also much UX design." Paul then says "yes indeed, most likely that which Buxton calls the holistic kind. Certainly, also, much focus on what we in the design business call, front-end design, which is where you will encounter this word, *Ideation*." And, something else too, for Julia has noted Mercedes Man's derogatory remarks about design thinking! So the intelligent observation is left for Julia, a woman to say: "some time ago it became evident that design had, for many reasons, become out-of-date, which is also the case for many ways of thinking, and that too much emphasis was being placed on back-end design, but with this acknowledged and understood, there came about a different approach, that which we now refer to as UX design." Obviously, this is way beyond the capabilities of image-making men and people in DG CONNECT to understand.

Looking from a different place and time, Julia and Paul review those questions that the panel are supposed to be considering, which mysteriously they seem to be either ignoring or just circling around, as they focus instead on pitching, as though in a competitive bidding process, to lay claim to be the partner of choice. And the audience too, obviously wishing to stake a claim to a share of the money, to the delusion, they also do contribute, with fine words of the kind that in another performance, were spoken to an emperor that many children, when very young, learned about in a very famous and iconic storyline.

And of these questions – How can the arts inspire creativity in general? How can spill-overs from creativity in the arts be harnessed by industry? How can spill-overs from creativity in the arts be harnessed by society? – Julia notes that no speaker has questioned them, and not even raised any concerns whether the way they are phrased suggests that DG CONNECT clearly does not understand and has learned nothing at all. So much for DG CONNECT's claim to be using art as a hammer! Probably they are, but to smash art!

So the performance draws to a close, but what is this? Julia it appears is making a note, writing down some words that one of the speakers spoke. She holds up her scrap of paper to Paul, and her mischievous smile appears once more, along with a wink, and for a moment Julia and Paul have become one, for evidently an idea for another episode in their surrealist performance has just be born, to deal with this very interesting statement: "… artists working on new technology for dance theatre, when brought into the brainstorming, came up with an idea that not a single scientist, engineer or designer could ever think of – projecting a virtual follow-me car on the windscreen and the driver just follows this virtual car …" Oh dear!

And of summing up, what should be said? It was clearly an empty session, not at all about art, and a complete waste of most peoples' time, and this stands in sharp contrast to the companion ICT 2015 performance known by the name *The Innovation Revolution: Creativity and Arts in ICT*, where much greater substance can be found, mostly because, the main focus was on what is termed the creative industries. Yet here too, strongly evident was the *Ideology of Creativity*.

Many questions also arise about whether what was being discussed in this other session was indeed art, or just artists working in other jobs, for it is indeed the case that not all those who from art school do graduate, follow careers as artists, but instead, to related jobs often do gravitate, so back once more to UX design! And just how imaginative and creative is all this? Julia and Paul ask this, for, without a doubt, even this session was framed within a well-defined and conventional mind-set with people saying very conventional things, through speaking of methodologies, intellectual property and such things. And clearly there was one who was very adept at pressing all the political buttons, who sang and danced so beautifully to the puppeteer's score – Brussels is full of such singing and dancing people, which is one of the problems. Julia and Paul call them the *Empty-headed Ones* – they who speak a lot but say very little of worth.

Yet there was one, who, among all this talk of creativity, and the posturing, and the sycophantic praising of the European Commission, and people silently saying, "hey look at me", clearly stood out from the grazing herd by not mentioning creativity, but instead, did of art speak, and in her presentation slides, even mentioned subjective knowledge, and in doing so, quietly established a credibility that no-one else did. And the name of this person is Laura Beloff, who clearly has more understanding than all the others combined.

Future generations will ask of this thing called STARTS, which Julia and Paul have noted is a manifestation of the *Ideology of Creativity* – why was it that so many people were so wrong?

Art, ICT and STARTS: DG CONNECT's post-action evaluation of ICT Topic 36 – Boost synergies between artists, creative people and technologists!

And now we overhear a conversation between Julia and Paul:

"Julia!"

"Yes Paul, xxx"

"Thanks. But what are you up to now you crazy artist? A post-evaluation of an activity when the Call for proposals has not even closed! The projects will not start until early 2017, and they won't be completed until 2019-20 at the earliest."

"Yes I know, it's great! Your problem is that you are too logical. You're far too bound-up in the notion of rationality and objectivity."

"Uncreative as well! Don't forget my creativity deficit."

"Indeed!"

"And I'm a man!"

"Well, so it seems! But don't you understand that an organisation that is spending eight million euros of public money, is over hyping and politicising a topic, clearly has some other agenda that involves instrumentalisation of art for dark political reasons, and, well, it's going to be a huge success this thing that they are STARTing. And having dragged-in those European Commissioners to say ridiculous things, no-one is ever going to admit that the whole thing has been a waste of public money because they did the wrong things. What we are seeing is manipulation that needs exposing for it demonstrates the true nature of the European Commission. So it's obvious that the topic is going to be amazingly successful."

"You're right of course. So what's your post-action evaluation?"

"Simple! STARTS has been a massive success. Synergies between (uncreative) technologists and (creative) artists have been boosted. We are overwhelmed by the number of unconventional and compelling products and services that have been produced. Silos have collapsed and amazing structured dialogues have resulted. The increase in the transfer of knowledge between the ICT and the creative industries is astonishing. The culture of the ICT sector has been transformed. At long last there is an appreciation of the societal and economic added value of creativity. And we have achieved a more innovation-oriented mind-set."

"Of course you're right. Now that the technocrats have committed to spending eight million euros they will have no choice but to proclaim STARTS as a massive success."

"Now Paul, you have a lot of experience of ICT product development and design, so tell me please how one can measure if a product is unconventional and compelling?"

"Good question Julia. The answer though, is not something that those caught-up in ICT Topic 36 ideology will want to hear, for it could take many years to determine just how compelling a product is. That it is unconventional might be easier to determine, but the world is full of unconventional products that failed to even make a glimmer of recognition, because thinking up new ideas for products is the easy bit. And if you doubt this, just watch Dragons' Den on BBC2.

"People who engage in technology joy-rides are developing unconventional products all the time, only to find that they have not thought about it sufficiently to even be worth considering for anything other than the *also ran* list in the history of potentially compelling product ideas. Ultimately what determines if something is compelling is the market, and that applies if one is selling something or giving it away free-of-charge through an open-source/Creative Commons model. But the chances of achieving this status are much improved by doing the right things at the right time, and one of the most critical phases is that which we call the *front-end* of design.

"The market is more likely to respond if at the front-end, important matters are properly considered such as concept development, industrial design, as well as the emotional dimension of design, interaction design, usability, and many other important issues, which today are all encompassed by holistic UX with its strong emphasis on front-end ideation. And to these critical issues one can add strategy and strategic vision, business models, timing, marketing, understanding of competing approaches or technologies, regulatory frameworks, social issues, barriers to adoption, …

"These are all things which those involved in the ICT commercial sphere, especially those working on consumer products, should know about and must today practice if they want to be successful. It's basic and largely not something that artists are familiar with. Self-evidently, judging by ICT 2015 conference performance *Driving Innovation through Creativity and the Arts*, it is largely also not something that DG CONNECT is familiar with as well.

"In that conference performance one can see some very bad examples of design concepts, which actually undermine some of the speakers' credibility and that of their organisations. Take the case of the car side window that is providing the child with in-vehicle edutainment. A compelling product idea? Not really. It is actually a very dangerous one. Someone in the audience noted that the child in the video was not wearing a seat belt which is illegal in the United Kingdom. But matters are worse than this, for just look at the child's posture, and how the child's torso, and hence its spine, is twisted. This is not a posture than anyone, child or adult, should be placed in. But this is not the worst of it! In the UK there is a law that requires children up to the age of 12, or until they reach a height of 135cm, to use a special car seat (restraint). Good quality ones are designed to provide some protection again side impacts. And the potential site of the side impact is the rear door and window, which is also the very place where the child is being invited to play. This is not good design, it's technology joyriding!

"So, one should ask why such a design was pursued to the stage demonstrated in the speaker's video clip. The speaker actually provided the answer to this question – they are caught-up in the *ideology of prototyping*, which is otherwise known as the road to making expensive mistakes.

"It's like being back in the early 1990s watching people talking about prototyping as though it is some form of panacea. It's actually a very dangerous and addictive drug that needs to be used with great caution."

"So Paul, the more we look into these matters the more foolish DG CONNECT look."

"Yes Julia. It's like turning over a stone – all sorts of things start wriggling and crawling about. And it is not a matter of DG CONNECT looking foolish, they are dangerous technocrats – ignorant, arrogant and incompetent. And fools and their money are easily parted and the phrase incompetence at the tax-payers expense comes to mind.

"The point I am making, is that if you are in the ICT sector and do not understand the basics of modern design practices, and are looking to DG CONNECT for assistance, then we have beyond doubt achieved a position where the blind are leading the blind. This is truly the *Road to Serfdom*. Post-evaluation over?"

"Not quite Paul. The silliness of all this creativity nonsense, clearly exposes, to those who care to look, a significant strategic weakness in Western thinking, which those who are not caught-up in Western ideologies, like the Chinese and the Indians, can exploit."

"Yes, Julia. Xerox PARC plainly understood though, for they clearly said of their Artist in Residence Programme that started in 1992, yes that's right, 1992, nearly 25 years ago – 'it's not about bringing creativity to ...' "

"The 1990s once more and your 25 year rule, Paul – the EC does the right thing only 25 years after it was the relevant thing to do! And it is indeed the case that bringing artists into research, development, and innovation processes is not about bringing creativity to scientists, engineers and technologists. Deficit thinkers, however, lacking understandings of the complexities of the matter, have no choice but to position artists in this way, for to do otherwise would undermine their ideologies and collective delusions. Oh, the delights of the fragmented and reductive mind, with its cognitive biases and its silent narratives – such minds speak so much about evidence-based policy making, about quantified knowing, but in reality they engage in behavioural policy making but do not realise this."

"It's that old question, 'Why so smart yet so stupid?' The answer to which, we know."

"Yes Paul, we do indeed. But there is more ..."

"More?"

"Yes Paul. More! The Call topic ICT 36 mentions in the expected impacts, silo-breaking. Robert Madelin also mentions this in an interview he gave just before he started his new job as Senior Adviser for Innovation. But it is clear that the European Commission, DG CONNECT and the ICT programme if they know anything about silo-breaking and why silos exist in Western culture, are making a very good job of hiding this understanding, for if they did know, they would certainly not have specified ICT Topic 36 the way it is. And I must say most artists and creative people also do not understand this issue. Why should they?"

"Because they're alchemists Julia!"

"Yes Paul, this seems to be how we are perceived. We are, as the Americans would say, the proverbial silver bullet. So more of that zone of discredited practice! Yet, I do know someone who does have knowledge and experience of silos."

"Yes, back once more to the early 1990s! And there are worse revelations yet to come Julia!"

"Oh yes indeed Paul, there is far worse to come. By the end, when this book is completed and then published, all those governments in other parts of the world, who might also be interested in bringing artists into research programmes, will have a reference model of what not to do – it's called the European Commission STARTS Platform, and ICT Topic 36. This is the price, DG CONNECT, that you will pay for not listening. Welcome, DG CONNECT to the nexus of Science, Technology and the Arts! Did no-one tell you about art and what it can do, and the notion of maintaining critical independence? Evidently not!"

So, as minds in DG CONNECT cross the frontier that marks the boundary between 1989 and 1990, and they begin to experience the 1990s, back in 2016 …

Art, ICT and STARTS: The European Commission in the form of DG CONNECT seeks artists to act as handmaidens to technologists

The European Commission, in the form of DG CONNECT, operating at the forefront of 1990s *Ideology of Creativity* thinking, is seeking artists to work with technologist, to bring creativity into ICT research, development and innovation processes, because DG CONNECT's new ideology is that technologists and engineers are not creative people, which just shows how much they understand – very little. Terms and conditions most definitely apply. Most importantly, be clear that you will be a handmaiden and you should know what handmaidens are expected to do.

Terry Fenton wrote about artists as handmaidens in a 1969 paper called *Two Contributions to the Art and Science Muddle: 1. Constructivism and its Confusions.* Why, you might ask, is this issue still relevant in 2016? The answer is provided by John Dewey, who, in 1920, wrote this:

"Surely there is no more significant question before the world than this question of the possibility and method of reconciliation of the attitudes of practical science and contemplative aesthetic appreciation. Without the former, man will be the sport and victim of natural forces which he cannot use or control. Without the latter, mankind might become a race of economic monsters, restlessly driving hard bargains with nature and with one another, bored with leisure or capable of putting it to ostentatious display and extravagant

59

dissipation." This is most definitely not about *two cultures* in the sense defined by C P Snow. It could however be about another story of two cultures – West and East.

Humanity has now become that monster, and scientists, technologists, engineers and mathematicians have become its handmaidens. DG CONNECT has decided that artists must now become handmaidens to the monster and help those other handmaidens in their quest to turn our planet into unconventional and compelling products, of which there are already far too many.

You will have noticed that in December 2015, the world's politicians meeting in Paris decided that they are not going to do anything about this thing called Global Warming. Instead, they have shifted responsibility for dealing with this problem, to our grandchildren, later this century. Cleverly they have reached agreement to do nothing, while being able to claim that they are doing something. So it is business as usual. And DG CONNECT are also contributing to this business as usual approach, and are appropriating art for political reasons, one of which has to do with its image and that of the European Commission – art wash!

In the report produced by the Los Angels County Art Museum about their Art and Technology Programme (late 60s & early 70s), they reflected on the reasons why industries participated. One of the identified reasons was companies trying to modernise their image. This is what DG CONNECT and the European Commission are doing – image making, because they have a very tarnished image and a poor track record, especially in DG CONNECT. They also do not understand very much about how to use art in research and worse, do not want to understand.

There is no such thing as a view from nowhere.

Art is the way to destroy this monster (and DG CONNECT) and to begin to construct a different civilisation – one that does not make a virtue of living life like a plague of locusts. So be aware when you join in with the STARTS circus, that you are becoming a handmaiden of the monster. And if you do join in, please become subversive, and make of DG CONNECT the fools that they are, for it is highly unlikely that they will recognise that, making them look like fools, is what you are doing. This is the power of art – artists can have very sharp teeth and can bite without those who have been bitten ever realising this.

Art, ICT and STARTS: DG CONNECT – Instrumentalisation warning

Continuing from the previous chapter, I now ask this question: What part of, *artists do not like to be instrumentalised*, DG CONNECT, did you not understand?

Instrumentalisation – to use people as a means of achieving an end. ICT Topic 36: Boost synergies between artists, creative people and technologists – the State, in the form of the European Commission's DG CONNECT, using artists as a means of achieving their ends. This is a sinister development and a foretaste of what to expect in the future as technocrats, deluded into thinking that they know what they are doing, appropriate anything and everything in the service of the power of money. Time to resist while you still can! And if you do participate in the *Tale of the Director General's New Clothes*, you cannot say that you were not warned! You too will stand there and proclaim that the very naked Director General is wearing the most exquisite suit of clothes. Such is the nature of self-constructed realities and collective delusion. It's money talking! This is the corrupting nature of the Brussels bubble – and a bubble it most certainly is, full of people out-of-touch with reality, living in the past. But judging by what one also sees elsewhere in the world of STEM, they are not alone.

Instrumentalisation of artists is wrong, but, self-instrumentalisation is not, that is to say, artists leading the move and developing their practice towards the use of art for more utilitarian purposes, which they have been doing since long before DG CONNECT arrived on the scene. And there are examples and lessons to be learned from this self-instrumentalisation. If you want to know more about this, we refer you to the ICT ART CONNECT study report. And there you will find what? Read it and find out for yourselves about all the well-known examples and the lessons that can be drawn from them that were – never studied. Now why was that? Of course you may yourself not be aware of these, which is why the study report should have mentioned them, so that known problems would not be repeated. But why bother with such details when the poor taxpayer is footing the bill for DG CONNECT's deluded adventure in wonderland.

The problem that we face is that the current drive to use art comes from people within the existing power structure and what is very clear is that they do not understand art and are just seeking to exploit it, often based upon restrictive cognitive biases, as well as STEM agendas, which lead to the positioning of art as a resource to be deployed in the service of those who hold power, i.e. those who have the money. This is often reflected in the words spoken by STEM people who advocate art-science and art-technology collaboration: it's all about using art for communication, visualisation and, more recently creativity. This is just like the old *artist-in-tow* model from the eighteenth and nineteenth centuries – "hey sketch and paint that plant please." This is not art. It is often also the case that those in STEM also are engaging in image making; the remaking of their own image to make themselves look more respectable – art wash! DG CONNECT serves to demonstrate the point.

The mind-set that treats art as just another way for STEM people to pursue their agendas and role as handmaidens is most definitely a subject for artistic study. There is plenty of material for satire, of the descriptive and the plastic form. This is like finding a diamond mine!

To tolerate instrumentalisation or not to tolerate instrumentalisation, that is the question: whether it be nobler in the mind to suffer the slings and arrows of outrageous fortune, or to take arms against a sea of troubles, and by opposing end them.

You might have already perceived that, in CONNECTing with STARTS, I have chosen to take arms, and my arms are the instrumentalisation of DG CONNECT. Do unto others as you would have done unto yourself! So now they are being used to serve my ends …

What are these ends? What are the results? Revelation, you will find, is a slow process of discovery. But if you are artists you will already know this.

If there is to be self-instrumentalisation, then those who hold power, i.e., those with the money, will have to surrender that power and allow the arts to take charge of how that money is used. The message is clear – The European Commission, DG CONNECT, and others, they have to go. There are other means of undertaking international projects, European or otherwise. Is there anyone out there listening? Now is the moment to learn from the DG CONNECT's nonsense and to begin to construct a different type of research and innovation system, one that is not founded in the past. Time to set Prometheus free! Skunk works!

There is more to bringing artists into ICT research and product development, than is dreamt of in DG CONNECT's and STEM's self-constructed and very limited reality …

And thanks to Will for allowing the use of his very elegant and poetic words, Julia xxx.

Art, ICT and STARTS: DG CONNECT and a 'baker's dozen' of reasons not to participate in a proposal to ICT Topic 36

If you are thinking such things as "if we're not in the race ..." or "it's worth a try ..." and other such foolish thoughts, here are 'baker's dozen' of reasons why they are foolish thoughts and you would be better devoting your energies to something more productive. I decided to do exactly this back in August 2014 and I have never looked back, and I was able to walk away because of experience, knowledge, and insights, which lead me now to highlight the following:

1. Be honest, you and everyone else are primarily interested in the money so what you will create is a marriage of convenience which is not the basis for a happy marriage. You might be lucky and find someone you do want to work with, but most likely you will be stuck with people and organisations who take more resources than they need, do very little in return, and who know little about the matter at hand. You will want a divorce.

2. Do you want to spend your time doing things that, you know are a waste of time, but some expert reviewing the project once it is up and running (if you manage to get one through the evaluation process) thinks that you should be doing, so that he (it is most often a man) can demonstrate his knowledge and that he is earning his review fee. Chances are he will not read all those useless paper documents that you will have to spend so much precious time writing.

3. Writing a proposal for an Innovation Action (IA) or a Coordination and Support Action (CSA) is very difficult and it is highly likely that you will not write a very good one. But even if you do …

4. Do you think that you proposal is going to be evaluated properly? Quite a delusion that you have! Chances are that it will not be properly evaluated, for all sorts of reasons: the wrong experts looking at it; their lack of experience in peer review; their cognitive biases; their hidden agendas; their misunderstandings that they should not be evaluating against that which they would wish to see; people who do not know the limits of their own knowledge, etc. Add to this some very basic yet common mistakes like experts not understanding the evaluation criteria, and, the sole expert with a negative view, out-of-step with the others, who, having decided that your proposal is weak, will drag down the consensus mark so that there is no chance of the proposal being funded.

5. The possibility that the Commission, a political organisation, have already decided who will be successful … surely you do not believe all that talk about proposals being fairly evaluated. Topics like ICT 36 are exactly the type where the Commission is most likely to manipulate the evaluation. Of course I must make clear here that this never happens! Strangely though, having been involved in more evaluations than I can count (the number is three digits), I know exactly how one can, if so inclined, *manage* the evaluation!

6. ICT Topic 36 is not research! It has been termed as *fiddling with technology*, which means that it is based on *end-of-pipe thinking* where everything is decided, you just get to look at it, make a few minor suggestions, and then everyone will dance around saying how marvellous ICT Topic 36 is. CSAs and IAs will consume your time in activities that are not research. The best you can hope for is that you might in the process find something of interest for later use. That research is not wanted says a lot about the mind-set and level of understanding of the people in DG CONNECT. Read the descriptions that define what constitutes legitimate activities for CSAs and IAs, and then compare these with what is expected from a Research and Innovation Action, and you will understand what I mean.

7. You are unlikely to be involved in art – more likely it is design that you will be participating in.

8. If you know anything about past initiatives that bring artists into industry or research projects, like Welcome Trust's Sciart, the LA County Arts Museum A&T programme, Xerox Parc, and so forth, you will know that none of the lessons that can be learned from these have been incorporated into ICT Topic 36 – you can see this from the wording. Look carefully for the words that reassure you that there is protection for the artists and that you will not be exploited and then just discarded. Do you want to lose the right to use your ideas in any way that you choose?

9. After close to three-and-a-half years of engagement with artists, DG CONNECT are still caught-up in the same

notions of users and technologists suffering from deficits – this is exactly what they said at the very beginning in 2012. They still also hold to the (just as stupid) notion that special people called artists have special powers to address these imaginary deficits. They have learned nothing, which is no surprise for the mind-set from the outset was that they have nothing to learn, and they knew what art should be used for. Do you want to be associated with such an ignorant and arrogant organisation?

10. You can also see from the Call Topic wording that DG CONNECT are caught-up in the notion of the *elitism of art*, with creativity being the preserve of a few *special individuals* called artists, and they think too that the *art object* has a *special status* which only people with money can own – the very things that many contemporary artists reject. DG CONNECT are the new wealthy patron of the arts!

11. You should know that organisations that start appropriating art for their own agendas also end by imposing on artists, restrictions on artistic freedom. Surely you do not think you are going to be allowed to do what you want if it does not fit with DGCONNECTivism?

12. So whatever happened to distributed authorship? STARTS was put together behind closed-doors, and the infamous study was undertaken by a chosen few, who must be very special indeed, for they obviously had discovered the truth. So tell me please the names of the advisory group? We know a few, from quotes in the report, but who are the people that advised DG CONNECT? Not exactly the reference model

of openness and transparency that the European Commission is trying to implement through things such as Science 2, etc.

13. The above is largely directed at people from the art world, but if you are a technologist you too should also be asking questions whether you should be engaging in ICT Topic 36. DG CONNECT have classified you as being one of the uncreative ones, not at all special in the way that artists are. This is insulting and completely wrong. It demonstrates also the contempt in which people, such as yourself, are held by this arrogant out-of-touch organisation. And this they have made very clear at every step of the way towards that which they decided upon over three years ago. One of the biggest problems that Europe's ICT sector faces is an organisation called DG CONNECT and companies that still want to engage with them. What to do about the problem that is DG CONNECT?

Our condolences if you find yourself in a position of having no choice but to apply. Fortunately we did not need to put up with DG CONNECT's nonsense and are not interested in obtaining a share of the eight million euro. And that, as they say, has made all the difference. And what a difference it turned out to be. What this is however, will only emerge very gradually. In the meantime you can participate in various collective delusions, of which there are many.

Art, ICT and STARTS: DG CONNECT and DG CONNECTivism

DG CONNECT last week issued a proclamation decreeing that all artistic work undertaken with its funding will be part of a new artistic movement that will be known as DG CONNECTivism. The basis for the new movement is the *Ideology of Creativity*. Artists practicing in this new movement will be limited in terms of the topics that they will be allowed to explore. Enforcement will be achieved through the proposal evaluation process where a committee, working behind closed-doors, will decide what will be supported. Monitoring for continuing compliance will be achieved through a process called project review, where another committee, again working in secret, will ensure that only that which complies with the manifesto of DG CONNECTivism will be allowed to continue.

And if all this sounds familiar, something heard in the past, and even today in places, then this is because it is a very familiar refrain. But you want the money! This reminds us that we must write our article about DG CONNECT, the Roman Catholic Church and the Soviet Communist Party.

Every honed blade needs its dull stone, otherwise the cutting edge would just be blunt metal, undifferentiated from other blunt implements, and not able to do that which needs to be done. Thank you DG CONNECT for being our dull stone.

Julia and Paul.

71

Art, ICT and STARTS: DG CONNECT and constraints

Constraints are parameters that guide processes and activities. They can be externally imposed such as through culture, deadlines or requests. They can be internally imposed unconsciously through developed beliefs and habits. They can also be consciously yet still internally devised to focus action towards specific goals that would not be explored in depth otherwise. Or they can be internally devised to ensure that matters that should be addressed are not! The design of constraints directly defines and confines a problem's search space, thereby provoking new and potentially creative explorations, or not, as is the case with DG CONNECT.

ICT ART CONNECT, otherwise known as STARTS, is the product of constraints, mostly those of the kind that are imposed unconsciously through developed beliefs and habits, but also, the constraints that come from a culture that *does not know what it does not know*, and an intention to exploit art for the European Commission's political reasons.

There are also another set of constraints at work, that rule out-of-order any thinking outside the limiting horizons of the European Commission's political agenda, which at its highest levels, in harmony with the policies of most of the Member State National Governments, is about abandoning the peoples of Europe to the power of money. Taken for granted here, are the neo-liberal agenda, with its defining features of global capitalism, economic inequality, environmental destruction, and cultural colonialism, where deviant cultures have to be converted to a secular and materialistic way of life through the imposition of European values. This is ultimate victory of Western Enlightenment thinking over anything that smacks of not being the rational and objective machine so much worshiped in the Western world, operating in the wider context of the economic machine, which exploits nature, another machine, in the cause of control and domination of people and nature. Recall John Dewey's monster!

Now is the time to resist, and to find a way to out-manoeuvre Europeans, for they surely have far too good an opinion of themselves and do not understand or respect those that are not European and do not want to be European. The opportunity now exits for the non-European world to exert itself, and to create the conditions which will also force Europe to stop being European. And if that happens then the planet and humanity will have a chance of surviving.

This is a moment for humanity to recognise that it is not seven billion individuals, but one living organism in which all people are connected together in ways that most Europeans do not understand, value, or even recognise. I am most definitely my brother's keeper, for I am my brother. When a child dies of famine in some forgotten poorly developed part of our planet, part of me dies too.

We are hyper-connected and always have been.

"Hey Julia, how did we get on to this subject?"

"Everything is connected Paul. Everything! Art is not just about gazing at aesthetically pleasing objects hanging on walls! It is also about confronting uncomfortable truths. And one of those uncomfortable truths is the reality of DG CONNECT – they are living in the past."

And speaking of the constraints and the past, next we will examine an aspect of DG CONNECT's past – a very specific constraint of the *not knowing* kind – which will come as a surprise to all those people, attending that ICT 2015 theatrical performance we wrote about a few chapters back, who thought that DG CONNECT was doing something new and timely. Déjà vu!

Art, ICT and STARTS: DG CONNECT and something old ...

Something old, something new, something borrowed, something blue.

Well it turns out that something old in DG CONNECT's case means that people from the arts have been involved with ICT research projects in DG CONNECT's past when it was called something else (as was the ICT Programme).

We are looking at project titles such as *Creating Aesthetically Resonant Environments in Sound*, and *The Educational Puppet Theatre of Virtual Worlds* and *Developing Collaborative Story Telling Environments for Children, with Children*. There is even a project with a partner called ZKM – you know who they are? Yes of course you do, they are the famous Centre for Media and Arts, where artists work with technologists.

So when Robert Madelin, at that ICT 2015 DG CONNECT theatrical performance, asked,

"How can the arts inspire creativity in general? How can spill-overs from creativity in the arts be harnessed by industry? How can spill-overs from creativity in the arts be harnessed by society?"

All he needed to do to find answers to these questions was to look back to the late 1990s and early 2000s and consult projects funded in Framework Programmes 4 and 5 under an initiative called Intelligent Information Interfaces (i3). To find out more about i3 and some of its art-driven projects, just look in the ICT ART CONNECT study report where you will find ... Oh dear there is no mention of i3! Now why is that we wonder?

Thus armed with such insights, along with knowledge of all those artists in industrial research lab initiatives (over the period from the 1960s to the early 2000s), and all those other art-science and art-technology programmes that have been and gone, combined with understandings of industrial and societal changes and needs, DG CONNECT might have been able to construct something that might have been useful. We say might, because one can never tell with technocrats, especially given that in another area, the social sciences, DG CONNECT are also engaging in another nonsense based on poor understanding of past work and future needs.

As for all those people at the ICT 2015 event praising the European Commission – what were they thinking saying such ridiculous things? Perhaps they were ... (Paul's note – Apologies but I have removed Julia's text!).

Now Commissioner Moedas is here and wishes to make an apology:

"When I said that more and more we all understand that innovation in the future will be on the intersection of arts and sciences, I was wrong, for which I apologise. What I should have said is that innovation in the past has been at the intersection of arts and sciences. What it will be in the future I have no idea and neither has DG CONNECT. Henceforth I will be sticking to my own portfolio, and will leave Commissioner Oettinger to speak DG CONNECT's words of nonsense. I wish him good luck for he will obviously need it."

Oh look Commissioner Oettinger is here as well. Is he going to apologise too?

"I want to say that the people writing this book, whoever they are – I do not understand who they are for all this surrealistic art is beyond me – are correct about artistic freedom which is why I have issued an imperial decree: No restriction on artistic freedom should be applied as it might compromise the creative process and thus, the essence of innovation as the valuable out-of-the-box thinking of artists is rooted in their artistic independence."

"Hi Commissioner! Yes it's me, Julia again. Glad to see that you have taken note of one tiny aspect of our critique, but still you persist with this *Ideology of Creativity* nonsense. You issue your decree because you have felt the breath of the tiger on your throat.

"What you did not say however, is how this artistic freedom is to be ensured – most likely because you do not know. And knowing DG CONNECT as we do, your words are worthless, as those who have experienced state interference in art in the past will testify.

"And already there is demonstrated a contradiction between your empty words and that which is DG

CONNECT's (supposed) open consultation. This comes far too late, being issued after the Call for proposals closed, after the evaluation has taken place, and after the projects to be funded have been selected by – we really do not know by whom! We think too that this consultation is a means of countering the obvious fact, that you did not, when it mattered, have an open consultation with the ICT industry and a wider circle of artists than those who around the trough did gladly position themselves. You act now to consult, in the belated understanding that people will know that DG CONNECT did silence the voices of artists, and in art history, DG CONNECT will be recorded as doing so. It is a pity that you did not see the email that was sent by a DG CONNECT official, following the opening of the *so called open consultation.* Oh dear, still up to your old European Commission tricks!

"As for exploring further the contradiction we leave you to find it for yourself, for as we have told you already, we will be telling you nothing. You won't see it – this we can promise you!"

DG CONNECT has stated that their STARTS circus is going to be rolled out across Horizon 2020! In other words, a further waste of public money! And few will raise objections because what most people want is to get their hands on public money. This is the nature of the moral corruption that now pervades Europe's research and innovation systems.

Here is an opportunity for the rest of the world to do things that are not circus acts. Artist-led research programmes with carefully selected foci, strategically driven to transform research and innovation systems, to transform STEM, to ...

We have given this matter much thought and to do that we first had to know the past and understand the future potential.

Art, ICT and STARTS: DG CONNECT and Maker Spaces

Before us, lying on the table, is the May 2015 copy of IEEE Spectrum Magazine. It is open at the page where there is an article about the growth of Maker Spaces in China and the support for Maker Spaces by the Chinese Ministry of Industry and Information Technology (MIIT), support which includes an online platform for makers to exchange information about projects.

Maker Spaces and maker culture, link to notions of hacker spaces, hacking culture, and the associated ethics and motivation. One might say that collectively these represent a growing cultural phenomenon of creative expression, playfulness, which are driven by more utopian ideals than society provides through its focus on selfish greed, which is the driver of Western capitalist economies past and present, which, clearly, an increasing number of people are dissatisfied with.

There is an interesting remark in this IEEE article, which relates to speakers (at the CESAsia 2015 contest) who represented the Chinese government. These people seemed to consider makers as nascent business entrepreneurs, and Maker Spaces as commercial incubators that would feed directly into industry. And there is this very interesting quote:

'But several speakers were quick to make the point that while commercial products can come out of Maker Spaces, it would be a mistake to view them, and the people working in them, so narrowly: "We try our best turn our creativity and hobbies into reality. We may be able to commercialize in some areas, but in others we are simply playful in our effort. Makers go beyond the scope of entrepreneurs in our effort," says Nanjing Maker Space's Zheng.'

So I am back to the question of DG CONNECT and their understanding of artistic practices in research, development and innovation, and indeed, whether they have appreciated the difference between creative expression and artistic expression, and also if they have appreciated that in Maker Spaces, there is a crossing of beliefs, for clearly there are artistic movements which also embrace the ethics and ideals of Maker Spaces. Collectively these are a part of a fundamental change away from the very economy and its beliefs that DG CONNECT is still immersed in, and to which it seeks to appropriate art to the service of (yet another example of their art-science muddle).

Artists therefore take note – if you participate in STARTS, history may well judge you to be out-of-step, and you might in the end be branded as being also, people who are living in the past. You could of course become subversive and hack STARTS from within, which is most definitely something that history will applaud, and if in the process of doing this, you relieve DG CONNECT of some of its money, that too would be a nice thing to do for poor artists – Robin Hood!

However, reality speaks a different story. Most of the EU money will be going to institutions that by their nature consume vast resources, and require resources to oversee the consumption of resources, and resources to acquire resources, so that resources can be consumed in overseeing the consumption of resources and acquiring more resources, which require resources ... And the – literally – poor artist will receive of this money taken from the rich, very little, for the reality of STARTS is that it has been hijacked by a small group of vested interests who seek only one thing – money – resources to feed the resource hungry institutions that consume resources ...

The good thing though is that the technocratic nonsense that is STARTS, reveals to the rest of the world how not to address art in research, development and innovation processes. And hacking ICT ART CONNECT now expands to a hack of Europe itself, through the enabling of its creative destruction, for now the weaknesses, flaws and moral corruption of the institution that is the technocracy known as the European Commission's DG CONNECT are revealed for all to see.

More to come! And more, and more... This is a book taking shape! And what a book it will be: STARTS – Science, Technology and the Arts. It will be an artistic examination of the life of DG CONNECT and its image making appropriation of art.

Art, ICT and STARTS: DG CONNECT and the Ideology of Creativity

The *Ideology of Creativity* – a false image, a collective delusion, a constructed reality: one that is more attractive than reality, which is that many activities that people are forced to participate in by patriarchal power structures, do not represent fulfilling and original work, but the execution of other people's timetables, plans and agendas, which involve blocking real creativity in the name of preserving a culture that makes a virtue of living life like a plague of locusts. Whatever name one gives to the *Ideology of Creativity* – ICT ART CONNECT, STARTS, STEAM or SEAD – they are still the *Ideology of Creativity*. No amount of CONNECTing, STARTing, STEAMing or SEADing will change this fundamental and uncomfortable truth. Unless one learns the lessons herein contained!

So now we have a definition of STARTS; knowledge of what the letters S, T, A, R and T actually mean: artists are forced, often because of lack of funding, to participate in a patriarchal power structure, where they will not be undertaking fulfilling and original work, but will have to implement other people's timetables, plans and agendas, with their artistic creativity blocked in the name of preserving a culture that makes a virtue of living life like a plague of locusts.

When you have finished reading this book, you will know what Stephen Wilson meant when he highlighted one role of the artist in science and technology as being that of critical practitioner: the deconstruction of cultural patterns of integrating science and technology to clarify underlying meanings ignored in the over-hyped flow of normal technological and commercial life. In the case of STARTS, there is much to deconstruct. And one thing you can be sure of is that DG CONNECT's feigned interest in art, most surely does not encompass critical practice. What *image seeking* exploiter of the arts would wish to become the subject of this type of artistic practice? Why would DG CONNECT, a failing public organisation, want to be the subject of satire and ridicule?

Back now to the *Ideology of Creativity*, which also reveals yet another strategic flaw in Western thinking, and those all important cognitive biases, that China, now ascending once more, can use to unleash the forces of creative destruction against the West. The people of the Western world proclaim their secularism, and sometimes even proudly announcing their atheism, but they are still *People of the Book*.

And when the Americans look at STARTS they will surely ask: where's the beef? By this we mean where is the evidence? What's that you say: "it's in the ICT ART CONNECT study report!" But we have read this several times and cannot find any evidence. There are of course some anecdotes, not just in the report, but spread across the globe in many places, but that which people call evidence is hard to come by. It is an interesting area that requires further investigation, both theoretical and empirical. But some evidence does not stand-up to close scrutiny. The words *disingenuous* and opportunistic come to mind! Back once more to that matter of moral corruption and spin.

This lack of evidence is why you, DG CONNECT, are now engaging in make-believe, inventing things, calling-on that that you do not understand, in the hope that you will not be found out. To which we say, *Wizard of Oz*!

Art, ICT and STARTS: DG CONNECT and the Wizard of Oz

Is this a poem?

> *STARTS*
>
>> *What STARTS*
>>
>> *The road to serfdom*
>>
>> *Is a technocratic failing*
>>
>> *CONNECTED with the past*
>>
>> *Which in DG CONNECT*
>>
>> *Can be found predominating*
>>
>> *So not in the present*
>>
>> *Nor the future*
>>
>> *Is it ever found operating*
>>
>> *Thus DISCONNECTED DG CONNECT*
>>
>> *Now stands condemned*
>>
>> *At the END*
>
> *ENDS*

What now follows is not a poem, but it is poetic:

DG CONNECT desperately searching for evidence. None found! "Never mind, we will still spend eight million euro of your money, for we will in the end just invite some of our experts to tell us what a marvellous thing STARTS was" – straight-out of the Soviet Communist party manual for running a technocratic state. Forget about reality – propaganda is everything.

Artists working in research, development, innovation and design projects; this is not the same thing as using art in these types of projects. To do that one does not necessarily need an artist to be involved! This is part of the reference model we are developing. There are other modes of operation that are also part of this. We are, once again, being too theoretical! And reaping the benefits!

And now for a little story:

"I am Oz, the Great and Terrible. Why do you seek me?"

They looked again in every part of the room, and then, seeing no one, Dorothy asked, "Where are you?"

"I am everywhere," answered the Voice, "but to the eyes of common mortals I am invisible. I will now seat myself upon my throne, that you may converse with me." Indeed the Voice seemed just then to come straight from the throne itself: so they walked towards it and stood in a row while Dorothy said:

"We have come to claim our promise, Oh Oz."

"What promise?" asked Oz.

"You promised to send me to paradise when the technologists became creative," said the girl.

"And you promised to remove silos," said the scarecrow.

"And you promised to produce unconventional and compelling products," said the Tin Woodman.

"And you promised to make European industry more competitive through working at the intersection of science, technology and the arts," said the Cowardly Lion.

"Are technologists really now creative?" asked the Voice and Dorothy thought that it trembled a little.

"Yes," she answered, "I gave them artist's creativity elixir mixed in with a bucket of water."

"Dear me," said the Voice, "how sudden! Well come to me tomorrow, for I must have time to think it over."

"You've had plenty of time already," said the Tin Woodman angrily.

"We shan't wait another day longer," said the Scarecrow.

"You must keep your promises to us!" exclaimed Dorothy.

The Lion thought that it might be as well to frighten the Wizard, so he gave a large, loud roar, which was so fierce and dreadful that Toto jumped away from him in alarm and tipped over the screen that stood in the corner. As it fell with a crash they looked that way, and the next moment all of them were filled with wonder. For they saw standing in just the spot the screen had hidden, a European Commission DG CONNECT official, with head full of strange ideologies and beliefs, who seemed as much surprised as they were. The Tin Woodman raised his axe, rushed towards the official and cried out, "Who are you?"

"I am Oz, the Great and Terrible", said the official in a trembling voice, "but don't strike me – please don't – and I'll do anything you want me to."

Our friends looked at him in surprise and dismay.

"I thought Oz was a knowledgeable Head, and knew about art", said Dorothy.

"And I thought Oz was a lovely Lady who knew how to use art to address patriarchal power structures in ICT research and innovation systems," said the Scarecrow.

"And I thought Oz was a terrible Beast that knew how to solve all the problems of the European ICT sector by using art in research and innovation," said the Tin Woodman.

"And I thought Oz was a Ball of Fire, that knew how to use art in research and innovation to sweep away the old and usher in a new golden era for the European ICT sector," exclaimed the Lion.

"No you are all wrong," said the official meekly. I am a technocrat who knows very little about all these things, and I have been making believe."

"Making believe!" cried Dorothy. "Are you not a great Wizard?"

"Hush my dear," he said: "don't speak so loud, or you will be overheard–and I should be ruined. I'm supposed to be a Great Wizard."

"And aren't you?" she asked.

"Not a bit of it my dear; I'm just a common man."

"You're more than that," said the Scarecrow, in a grieved tone; "you're a humbug."

"Exactly so!" declared the official, rubbing his hands together as if it pleased him. I'm a humbug."

"But this is terrible," said the Tin Woodman; "how shall we ever produce unconventional and compelling products?"

"Or make European industry more competitive through working at the intersection of science, technology and the arts?" asked the Lion.

"Or remove silos," wailed the Scarecrow, wiping the tears from his eyes with his coat sleeve.

"My dear friends," said Oz. "I pray you not to speak of these little things. Think of me, and the terrible trouble I'm in at being found out."

"Doesn't anyone else know you're a humbug?" asked Dorothy.

"No one knows it but you four – and myself," replied Oz. "I have fooled everyone so long that I thought I should never be found out. It was a great mistake my ever letting you into the Throne Room ..."

Thanks to L. Frank Baum for writing a children's story that, like Hans Christian Anderson's *The Emperor New Clothes*, speaks of the nonsense of human behaviour and DG CONNECT's STARTS initiative. We call it *behavioural policy making* – the delusion that people know what they are doing and that they are acting in a rational and objective way – humbug!

Art, ICT and STARTS: DG CONNECT, art-science, art-technology and POWAQQATSI

From the film POWAQQATSI:

po.waq.qa.tsi (from the Hopi language, powaq sorcerer + qatsi life) n., an entity, a way of life, that consumes the life forces of other beings to further its own life.

This is what DG CONNECT, what scientists, what technologists will try to do to art – they will try to consume it to further their own ideology and dogma. It has already STARTED … The SEADs are sown … The process is STEAMing ahead.

STEM driven art-science and art-technology practices: STEM consuming art to further its own life – POWAQQATSI.

And while they go about consuming life forces, do you think that they are going to be paying artists at STEM salary rates?

We will show those who are still able to listen how to do something completely different, but this thing that we reveal, it will be a heresy to those from the Western world, but not to those of the mysterious East.

It is time for *Chinese Solutions*! How are you feeling now all you *Vainglorious Enlightened Ones*? President Xi Jinping of the People's Republic of China already knows that it is time for *Chinese Solutions*! How are you feeling now all you *Vainglorious Enlightened Ones*?

Art, ICT and STARTS: DG CONNECT and those unconventional and compelling products

Once more we listen in on a conversation between Julia and Paul:

"Hi Julia, I see you have a book there about art, science and technology."

"Hi Paul xxx. Yes, indeed I do."

"*Art + Science Now: How scientific research and technological innovation are becoming key to 21st century aesthetics*, by Stephen Wilson. What's it about?"

"Well Paul, it's full of pictures and short descriptions of art made with science and technology."

"So it's also full of unconventional and compelling products?"

"No Paul, it is not. It's full of what could be art. Whether all is art is impossible to say, but it's a book about art, because that's what artists do – make art. They do not, in general, create unconventional and compelling products, for such things are part of world known as design, unless you think of the work of artists like Jeff Koons in that way."

"I see that Arduino is one of the art objects included. Surely that's an unconventional and compelling product. The book says that this was developed by an international consortium of artists."

"Well it's certainly used by artists, but also by maker communities, which are not necessarily the same thing."

"And home hobbyists as well."

"Yes, but the statement that it was developed by an international consortium of artists does not exactly tally with what is said elsewhere, for example in the book *Participation is Risky*. In that book the authors say that it was developed at an Interaction Design Institute in Northern Italy that teaches design students in new emerging fields of design intersecting with computer science and engineering. The teachers faced a problem that available programming boards were expensive and exoteric with difficult to learn programming languages. So they developed their own programming board."

"That word again Julia – design! And the relationship between art and design! A matter worth *exploring* at some future time, I think."

"Yes Paul, design, not art, but as you say, a relationship worth *exploring*! And by CONNECTING with organisations like the *Helen Hamlyn Centre for Design* at the Royal College of Art, DG CONNECT could have ... Well we will never know that they could have done. The desire to reconstruct their image was everything, hence the CONNECTION with art, and DG CONNECT once again damage European industry at taxpayers' expense.

"So Paul, back to Arduino, and its development by academics to teach their students. A plausible explanation?"

"It is certainly plausible Julia, for academics often do that – they are a maker community too! I have seen this is several university engineering departments. And of course in this specific case there is now a dispute among the founders about ownership of the Arduino name, and the issue of the rather underhand way that one of them registered it without telling the others."

"Indeed. Not exactly a paragon of openness, open innovation, and open-source."

"So, Julia, Raspberry Pi! That too is an unconventional and compelling product created by artists?"

"Why not, because it seems we are now in the realms of all sorts of nonsense and fantasy, thanks to DG CONNECT, and we are now entering that zone of discredited practice. It will set back the serious participation of artists in research by decades."

"Certainly in the West it will. I know too well what the likely reaction will be in US funding agencies. But there are new players in the game now, with different rules."

"You mean countries like China and India?"

"Yes Julia I do. These are not like the *Vainglorious Enlightened Ones*, and they know full well that most people in the Western world do not understand their cultures, or respect them or value them. So these non-European cultures have the potential to become a competitive weapon that can be used to unleash the forces of creative destruction against the West."

"So Paul, we live in interesting times!"

Art, ICT and STARTS: DG CONNECT's delusions and the new artist-led company called the Ideology of Creativity Inc.

Following on from our chapter on those unconventional and compelling products that special people called artists are going to create for DG CONNECT, Julia and Paul, the highly schizophrenic artist-technologist pairing, are proud to announce the launch of their new commercial venture which will be known as *Ideology of Creativity Inc*. This is an artist-led company dedicated to making the dreams of technocrats come true, by pandering to their delusions through the use of art to solve all those deficits that explain Europe's declining economic circumstance – explain that is, only if you are caught-up in the STEM way of knowing the world and creating reality which is very Ancient Greek in its orientation (patriarchal; elitist; disparaging towards manual work; intolerant of that which does not conform with the normal; contemptuous towards people who are not Hellenic (those people otherwise known by the Ancient Greeks as the untermenschen that were the barbarians); inclined towards achieving genetic purity through the practice of eugenics implemented through infanticide ...).

Together we will innovate at the nexus of science, technology and the arts. We will create business models for art-technology collaborations, invent and use common work practices to develop unconventional and compelling new products, navigate the valley of death, and participate in

START competitions in the quest to win one of those truly amazing and much sought after prizes – it remains to be seen it they mean cash in our pockets with no strings attached!

We have identified many areas where our very special products can be used to address deficits. We will be presenting our first product launch in the coming months. We can guarantee that our first product will save research funding agencies millions in unnecessary expenditure of public money on art-technology collaborations, for we have truly found a world beating solution, a panacea, to the creativity deficit. Watch this space for details of this astonishing silver bullet – this amazingly unconventional and compelling product!

Julia and Paul.

Art, ICT and STARTS: Hacking DG CONNECT's STARTS through ICT ART CONNECT DISCONNECT

ICT ART CONNECT (or STARTS) is something we have been following, monitoring and analysing since 2013, and on our web site (See Appendix: web link #3) we have archived most of the public-domain material to ensure that it is available for use by art historians and anyone else who wishes to make use of it, e.g. research funding agencies who want to avoid the catalogue of incompetence and unethical conduct that is DG CONNECT's STARTS initiative. Unlike DG CONNECT, all those other public research funding agencies that may have an interest in deploying art in STEM related research, will be constrained in their actions by fiduciary responsibility, and will have to exercise due diligence. This is one of the motivations for our hacking activities – why make any mistakes when DG CONNECT has made them all so that you do not have to! We also have other objectives.

This hacking, we have given a name – we call it ICT ART CONNECT DISCONNECT.

The hacking of ICT ART CONNECT (and STARTS) means the creative misuse of ICT ART CONNECT as part of a larger process of developing something known as *Art Practice as Research* with a view to developing it into something that can fundamentally change Western science and as well as achieving something that we call *innovating the innovation process*. We observe artists working with STEM people and note what they say, claim, and so forth. Interesting, but not in the sense that they would mean!

We learned long ago however that transforming Western STEM, is one of the greatest heresies that anyone can utter in the modern, so-called, but, in reality, not very, Enlightened world. But we care not. It serves our purpose very well to create these subjective and irrational emotional responses – this, after all, is one of the things that art can do. And bringing the subjective, the irrational and also the spiritual into Western STEM is what we are about. How are you feeling now?

ICT ART DISCONNECT is also part of the process we are undertaking to develop something we term scriptovisualism – this has clear links to feminist art for sure, but we go far beyond what this term originally meant. Probably we will not however be saying much more about this for the time being. It will be the subject of further books.

And as the results of this hack accumulate, the pieces of the jigsaw, long hung, unplaced and, unused, begin to assemble themselves as though by guiding hand into a theory that DG CONNECT will never understand.

We are being too theoretical once again. Of course we are, because theory is everything and not just art and literary theory, but other theories as well. Theory provides a cross-disciplinary explanation, theory provides the basis for an interdisciplinary transfer from one field to another, but most importantly, theory provides the keys to open the doors to transcendence – transcending disciplines to create the transformational ...

Art, ICT and STARTS: Art lesson – DG CONNECT's advice on involving artists in research programmes

Based on DG CONNECT's experience of ICT ART CONNECT and STARTS, this is how you involve artists in research programmes:

For this recipe you will need a failing institution that pays lip service to fiduciary responsibilities, and is willing to spend public money as part of its image making political agenda, e.g. the European Commission, represented by DG CONNECT, and its ICT research programme. You will also need some willing accomplices, who are either unaware of what you are doing or do not care. Important to this mixture are technocrats with an interest in art, but who do not know a lot, for a little knowledge is most certainly always a dangerous thing. Add to this list of ingredients a pre-determined agenda and some words about being open and willing to listen and to learn, accompanied by the body language that makes clear that this is not the case. Also important are the following ingredients: neo-liberalism; a failing European economy; and a bureaucracy that needs to justify its own existence, even at the price of Europe's economic wellbeing. Disregard the conflicts that these imply.

Now for the secret ingredient – political pressure from several sources demanding change, which will plant in your mind the notion of sucking from the arts, in a parasitic way, the credibility and kudos that they still retain, for on the whole, artists have not yet sold themselves to the power of money. This is obviously now in the process of changing as STEM people exercise their hegemony over research funding, and begin to bring the arts to bear on addressing their traditional agendas.

Optional at this point is trying to make yourself seem knowledgeable by referring to that technocrat called CP Snow – disregard all the critiques of this man and his poorly informed simplistic opinions, which were just the product of a fragmented and reductive mind (part of the problem).

Mix the above together and cook very slowly over many years. Make much noise! At some point in the cooking process add a special study which seeks to explore predefined sinister themes such as using art to *help more gracefully embed science and technology in society.* Make sure that the study is undertaken by people who are not going to be excluded from participating in the Call for Proposals that you already know will result, when the topic you have already decided upon is included in the work programme – then set-up an advisory group on the same basis. Whatever you do, you must not involve the ICT industry. Disregard all previous relevant activities that have been undertaken over the past 20 to 50 years. Take advantage of those allegedly morally corrupt relationships that the former Chief Scientific Advisor to a former President of the European Commission identified as existing between the European Commission and the experts that it uses. Moral corruption in the form of conflicts of interest, and a desire to obtain public money, are wonderful at

101

delivering that which you want. Whatever you do during the cooking, do not apply due diligence procedures to verify that what you have cooked is indeed the dish that is needed, otherwise you will not be able to eat that which you have already determined is going to be on your menu.

When you find that there is no evidence to support your sole truth, do not worry. The last thing you should do when you have dug yourself into a deep hole is to stop digging. Carry on digging regardless and START making random quotes taken from miscellaneous artists. Drop in a few buzzwords, like transdisciplinary, and refer to issues addressed in the 1990s, like silos. Few, like yourself, will know what you are talking about, so you have little to worry about. Refer to Steve Jobs and Apple, but whatever you do, do not seek to understand what he was saying back in 1996 about the liberal arts. Do not find out how Apple, and many other companies in the ICT sector (including the European ones), who produce consumer-facing products, go about developing their products.

Once the cooking is complete, enjoy the consequences, for when you sow the wind, you will mostly certainly reap the whirlwind. But you are a European, and a technocrat, so you do not understand this.

And for those of you in the European Parliament – is it not about time that you took action to stop these types of technocratic and morally corrupt practices? Or are you too caught-up in delusions? You are, for we have observed you also!

Surely it is time to do something about the problem that is DG CONNECT? And now you also know why the UK is leaving the EU – it was a choice between technocracy (remain a member) and democracy (leave), and the main argument for remaining was about money – the power of money once again! Have you not read Jürgen Habermas' critique of the European Union (especially the European Commission) – *The Lure of Technocracy*?

Some may have read Hayek's 1944 book *The Road to Serfdom*, which is a critique of – actually, organisations like the European Commission, which has already built *The Road to Serfdom*. And it uses the money that it takes from European citizens, via their National Governments, to keep the serfs in line. It has created a dependency culture, whereby it decides what it will do, and then it seeks experts, all of whom will benefit from the Commission's proposals, to support these plans. Then it often uses these experts to confirm that the money has been well spent. Dissenters are not tolerated and are sent into exile – i.e. they are dismissed as suffering from some deficit and never invited back. ICT ART CONNECT – the STARTS Platform – is a prime example of this form of technocratic corruption, which is one of the reasons we created this book.

Art, ICT and STARTS: Whitechapel Gallery, Electronic Superhighway, and DG CONNECT

One more time we listen in on a conversation between Julia and Paul:

"So Julia, we had a nice time when we visited the Whitechapel Gallery's exhibition, Electronic Superhighway 2016-1966."

"Yes that's right, Paul."

"Lot's of electronic, computer and digital art."

"Yes that's right, Paul."

"Many contemplative exhibits and much ambiguous communication, but, I note, no unconventional and compelling products."

"Yes that's right, Paul."

"Of course it is possible to consider the product of artists work as products, as in *device art*."

"Yes that's right, Paul."

"And a response to such thinking can be found in a work of art called *Animal Farm*."

"Yes that's right, Paul."

"But we do know of some unconventional products that were developed from works of art."

"Yes that's right, Paul."

"And we know why that happened."

"Yes that's right, Paul."

"Roy Ascott's Change Painting was one of the exhibits we saw."

"Yes that's right, Paul."

"Interesting aesthetics this painting, this work of art, this contemplative object."

"Yes that's right, Paul."

"A painting, in an exhibition about the electronic superhighway!"

"Yes that's right, Paul."

"All far too theoretical for DG CONNECT."

"Yes that's right, Paul."

Art, ICT and STARTS: DG CONNECT Gradgrinding the arts

"Bitzer," said Thomas Gradgrind. "Your definition of an artist."

"Highly creative special person. Uses ICT to make art objects, the sole purpose of which is utility – the utility of unconventional and compelling products. Works with uncreative technologists to provide corrections for their creativity deficit. Makes industry more innovative and therefore more competitive. Solves the problems that DG CONNECT imagines exits in the world of ICT. Breaks down silos. Uses special powers to embed ICT more gracefully in society. Does not require paying on equal terms with technologists. Will work for a pittance. Will even work free-of-charge. Someone to award prizes to, so that DG CONNECT's image is enhanced at public expense. Someone to be exploited by a technocratic, unaccountable, self justifying, European, bureaucratic organisation. Sole purpose is to serve DG CONNECT's image making agenda."

"Now European citizen number twenty," said Mr. Gradgrind, "you know what an artist is."

Thanks to Charles Dickens for giving the world, Mr Gradgrind. Yet again we find in the world of literature, a parody that reveals the true nature and behaviour of DG CONNECT. And if this makes them look like fools, that is because ...

Next a poem about DG CONNECT! Well you wanted to work at the nexus of Science, Technology and the Arts, and we so much want to use art to explain to those outside Europe how not to use the arts. It is an art project leading to a very unconventional and compelling product.

Art, ICT and STARTS: a poem about DG CONNECT and STARTS

Here is a poem:

"They dance around in a ring and suppose,
But the Secret sits in the middle and knows."

Many thanks to Robert Frost for wring the poem that in few words sums up DG CONNECT technocrats and their collaborators – predominantly men (no surprises!) – and all the supposing upon which STARTS is based – and by implication, also SEAD and STEAM.

Too much dancing around and supposing in STARTing, SEADing and STEAMing! Far too much! And to those who discover the Secret, the future belongs.

And yes, we have slightly modified Robert's original words.

Julia: the feminist artist part of the art-technology pairing that is – Julia and Paul (boosting synergies between artists and technologists, breaking down silos, correcting creativity deficits, and creating unconventional and compelling products and services!)

Art, ICT and STARTS: DG CONNECT and Pepper's Ghost

Artists are not in the business of unambiguous communication. Thus:

Collaborate

1. work jointly on an activity or a project. 2. cooperate traitorously with an enemy.

Binary

1. relating to, composed of, or involving two things.

Opposite

1. situated on the other or further side when seen from a specified viewpoint.

Dichotomy

1. a division or contrast between two things that are or are represented as being opposed or entirely different.

Imbricate

1. arrange (scales, sepals, plates, etc.) so that they overlap like roof tiles.

Hybrid

1. the offspring of two plants or animals of different species or varieties; 2. a thing made by combining two different elements.

Integrate

1. combine (one thing) with another to form a whole; 2. bring (people or groups with particular characteristics or needs) into equal participation in or membership of a social group or institution.

Nexus

1. a connection or series of connections linking two or more things; 2 a central or focal point.

Crossing

1. a place where roads or railway lines cross.

Connect

1. bring together or in contact so that a real or notional link is established.

Reality

1. the state of things as they actually exist, as opposed to an idealistic or notional idea of them; 2.the state or quality of having existence or substance.

Bureaucrat

1. An official in a government department, in particular one who is in particular perceived as being concerned with procedural correctness at the expense of people's needs.

Technocrat

1. an exponent or advocate of technocracy, a member of a technical elite.

Incompetence

1. inability to do something successfully.

Delusion

1. an idiosyncratic belief or impression maintained despite being contradicted by reality or rational argument, typically as a symptom of mental disorder.

Masculine

1. having qualities or appearance traditionally associated with men.

Denial

1. the action of denying something.

Patriarchal

1. relating to or denoting a system of society or government controlled by men.

Image

1. a representation of the external form of a person or thing in art; 2. the general impression that a person, organization, or product presents to the public.

Pretend

1. behave so as to make it appear that something is the case when it is not.

Projection

1. an estimate or forecast of a future situation based on a study of present trends; 2. the presentation of an image on a surface, especially a cinema screen; 3. the presentation or promotion of someone or something in a particular.

Illusion

1. an instance of a wrong or misinterpreted perception of a sensory experience.

Rationalise

1. Attempt to explain or justify (behaviour or an attitude) with logical reasons, even if these are not appropriate.

Construct

1. build or make something.

Constraint

1. a limitation or restriction.

Bias

1. inclination or prejudice for or against one person or group, especially in a way considered to be unfair.

Boundary

1. a line which marks the limits of an area; 2. a dividing line.

Convention

1. way in which something is usually done.

Humbug

1. deceptive or false talk or behaviour:

C P Snow

Smoke and Mirrors

DG CONNECT

Pepper's Ghost ...

Art, ICT and STARTS: DG CONNECT and STEM peoples' intention to use art to manipulate public opinion

"To help to more gracefully embed science and technology in society."

As soon as I heard this I recognised the sinister implications of what DG CONNECT wanted to use art for – to manipulate the public into accepting whatever scientist and technologists create. This is something one would have expected to hear in Moscow, in the Soviet Union, in the past, but we hear it from Brussels, from the European Commission, in the present. And also in many other places as well, all of which are part of the STEM world. The monster that John Dewey wrote about in 1920 has arrived!

Let us be clear – this statement about more gracefully embedding science and technology in society is one of the reasons why DG CONNECT is interested in art. This is a matter of public record, and to ensure that this is not forgotten is one of the reasons why I created the online ICT ART CONNECT archive (see Appendix: web link #3). DG CONNECT's other reason is image making, for they have a very tarnished image. And it is also now a matter of public record that many artists and arts organisations did collaborate with DG CONNECT. Their names too are recorded in the archive.

In one of my blogs, the one that goes by the title *When a Distinguished Professor of Art and Technology asks questions* ...(see Appendix: web link #4), I mentioned that some STEM people, from very prestigious institutions, had made very clear that their intention is to use art to manipulate the minds of the public into accepting science and technology – the true meaning of *more gracefully embedding*.

It is a truly Orwellian vision that these STEM people have! The phrases they use are: "When the emotions are targeted, individuals pay more attention to a particular event and commit to the cause, storing information in their long-term memory" and "... psychological ambiguity, in which the basic ideas and norms are broken down or weakened, and this disorientation allows individuals to reposition their points of view" and "the incorporation of art into communication of technology can promote new ways of considering issues, appeal to emotions, and form a celebratory atmosphere."

I have been warning for some time that STEM people's interest is using art is not benign. But mostly what I hear are STEM people and their *artists in residence*, creating a *celebratory atmosphere* that is likely to leave both groups with tarnished reputations, and titles such as *distinguished* looking somewhat empty. Enthusiastic but naïve practitioners! Enthusiasm though is dangerous and no substitute for critical thinking. Thus do the art-science and art-technology mutual admiration societies create the zone of discredited practice! And thus do I take up the pen ...

I refer people to the second definition of collaborate that I provided in the previous chapter.

You will pay a heavy price by becoming involved with DG CONNECT and all those STEM people itching to use art to restore their tarnished image and to manipulate the public so that the STEM world's techno-science delusions and technocratic intentions can become a reality. But there is a pen waiting here, and as I said in the blog *When a Distinguished Professor of Art and Technology ask questions:* "the pen is far mightier that the Scanning Electron Microscope and other such boy's toys."

Thus the artistic voices that DG CONNECT silenced, will be heard, and people will know that DG CONNECT did silence these voices.

Quietly and slowly, determination to expose the true nature of DG CONNECT and their collaborators will pay-off in the end. And the critique becomes a book with the title: *STARTS – Science, Technology and the Arts: The artistic voices that DG CONNECT silenced.* A British Library Cataloguing-in-Publication record has already been generated. The publication date is set for October 1st 2016. And from the critique came forth …

The next book, even stranger than this one, is already taking shape, in which STEM people who think they can appropriate art, the very ones mentioned above, encounter people – monsters – from the recent past who are somewhat *interested* in these STEM people and what they can do to help them create a *celebratory atmosphere*! And we are just warming-up! We are warming up and preparing – a reconnaissance in force!

115

Art, ICT and STARTS: DG CONNECT and this is not Art

And now we listen in on another conversation between Julia and Paul:

"Hi Julia"

"Hello Paul. You're cute. xxx"

"Um! Nice. But what are you looking at Julia?"

"It's a web page with a video clip called *Painting the Way to the Moon*," (See Appendix: web link #5).

"I see, and what's that you have there. It's very colourful."

"Indeed it is. It's a preliminary sketch that's all. It's called *This is Not Art* (See Appendix: web link #6). Do you understand?"

"Yes I do for you have taught me well. But will anyone else understand?"

"A good question Paul! A very good question indeed. It's all about theory."

Art, ICT and STARTS: DG CONNECT and 'they saw you coming'

Harry and Paul is a BAFTA Award-winning British comedy sketch show, first transmitted by the BBC, starring Harry Enfield and Paul Whitehouse.

I saw you coming is a sketch in which a Notting Hill antiques shop salesman (Enfield) sells junk to gullible wealthy women (usually portrayed by Sophie Winkleman) for extortionately large quantities of money.

ICT Topic 36 Boost synergies between artists, creative people and technologists or, as it should more correctly be described, *they saw you coming*, is a farce in which antiques salesmen (they are of course mostly men) sell well-known ideas and concepts from the 1990s and earlier (1960s), to willingly gullible technocrats (who are mostly men) for extortionately large quantities of public money, to bolster the image of a failing technocratic institution firmly planted in the past.

Meanwhile in places like China, India, and other parts of the non-European world, the obsession of DG CONNECT with Western notions of creativity is duly noted along with their significantly restrictive cognitive biases and lack of knowledge, leading to ... By the time the European technocrats discover this, approximately in 2035, it will be too late. Decline and Fall, a comedic novel by Evelyn Waugh.

The artist John Whitney was a pioneer is the use of computers in art, receiving support from IBM to pursue this work. In his 1980 book Digital Harmony: On the Complementarity of Music and Visual Art, he said:

"At some time in the mid-sixties *ad hoc* committees within the art world were being formed to sponsor art and technology. I was immediately elated: my creative needs might be recognised and fulfilled. Then, just as quickly, I was discouraged by obtuse, confused, or empty attitudes that developed among people of influence. Excitement grew over projects that were formulated with bandwagon haste around this subject. As a fad that came and went, along with so many others of that decade, the art-technology boom left in its wake as much prejudice as enlightenment."

He was writing about STARTS 36 years before STARTS.

Now Commissioner Moedas wants to speak:

"Yes indeed. I would like to repeat the point that I made in 2015 – I strongly believe that the time has come for a European initiative on research integrity."

You are correct, for an ethical meltdown is underway in the world of STEM, but few people want to talk about it. So, Commissioner Moedas, put your own house in order first. START with STARTS! Or will you engage in ethics wash in addition to art wash?

With all my love, Julia, xxx

Art, ICT and STARTS: Artist's creativity elixir – DG CONNECT's first unconventional and compelling product

Julia and Paul, operating at the nexus of science, technology and the arts, under the strict intellectual property regime of *Ideology of Creativity Inc* – all rights are reserved – are proud to present the first unconventional and compelling product to result from the European Commission's DG CONNECT STARTS Platform.

The product is known by the name Artist's Creativity Elixir. Further details can be found at Cheshire Henbury's web site (See Appendix: web link #7).

Yes, it is Artist's Creativity Elixir and not Artists' Creativity Elixir. Think about it!

Art, ICT and STARTS: DG CONNECT and another story of woe

This is a nursery rhyme:

> *I'll tell you a story*
> *About Jack a Nory;*
> *And now my story's begun;*
> *I'll tell you another*
> *Of DG CONNECT;*
> *And then my story,*
> *Will not be done,*
> *Because later I will,*
> *Tell you another ...*

This is a very European Commission story:

A long, long time ago when I was much younger than now ...

It was the 1980s and Information Technology (IT) was the big thing, and in manufacturing there was much interest in Computer Aided Design, which although not new, received a lot of research funding from national administrations and the European Commission. The European Commission continued with this support into the 90s and 00s as well.

One of the things that I noted about this research and the resulting systems was that they were entirely focused on supporting what in the design world is called the *back-end* – that's the place where the detailed engineering design is done and eventually finished. Yet many people knew that most of the costs involved in design solutions, and the place where expensive mistakes are often made, and where novelty is introduced, lies in the *front-end* of design. This was not an area where the IT world ventured.

In 1996 I was commissioned to write a management report by the Financial Times. They asked me to communicate to senior managers and executives in the automotive industry, the what, why and how of what was then called rapid prototyping (layer manufacturing) as it related to design and new product development. I was asked to do this in a way that non-experts would understand and to focus on business and implementation matters.

I told them that they had picked the wrong subject and that they should be producing a report about IT and its use in the *front-end* of design and new product development in the automotive industry. They did not believe me, but they were sensible and wise enough to check with their target audience – the senior managers and executives in the global automotive industry. The answer came back – most definitely this was a product that these people wanted.

And so I was commissioned to research and write this report. It was a sensitive subject. Not even the Financial Times brand name would get me through the barriers that went up when the automotive giants learned what I was doing. Ford in America issued a decree, from Vice President level, that no-one in Ford's new product development centres should talk to me.

But I did not need to – I know how to find out about that which I write about, and in the end a report that went by the name *Revolutionising New Product Development: A Blueprint for Success in the Global Automotive Industry* was published by FT. It was, as they say, a best seller.

So from 1996 we now move forward to 2006, and I am commissioned by DG CONNECT's predecessor, DG INFSO, to be a rapporteur for a consultation workshop in preparation for the workprogramme for the IST (now called ICT) research programme in FP7. And what was the subject of this consultation? Yes that is right, ICT for the *front-end* of design!

Better late than never, you might say. Not really, for nothing happened until 2010. One day while acting as a rapporteur for the *Factory of the Future Public Private Partnership*, I was informed by a DG INFSO project officer that the topic which had been discussed in 2006 would be included in the new workprogramme. So this is the timescale: issue a call, people write proposals, evaluation of proposals takes place, the results are known, the contracts are negotiated with the successful projects, and then the research projects can start – already it is early 2012! Three years later, you might have some results, already it is 2015! Back in 1996 I knew that this was a topic that needed research and that there was an opportunity for the ICT sector. DG INFSO/DG CONNECT clearly did not.

In the autumn of 2010 I carried out a mid-term review of a Marie Currie Initial Training Network project where I discovered that the issue of using ICT in the *front-end* of vehicle design had been addressed by the automotive

122

companies, and they were no-longer unwilling to talk about the issue.

This raises interesting questions about the relevance of research funded by the European Commission!

So what purpose DG CONNECT?

Art, ICT and STARTS: DG CONNECT and yet another story of woe

This is a nursery rhyme:

> *I'll tell you a story*
> *About Jack a Nory;*
> *And now my story's begun;*
> *I'll tell you another*
> *Of DG CONNECT;*
> *And then my story,*
> *Will not be done,*
> *Because later I will,*
> *Tell you another ...*

This is a very European Commission story:

And now it is 2004, and one more time I am commissioned by DG INFSO to be a rapporteur. This time it is for a high-level group called ISTAG – the Information Society Technologies Advisory Group. The task is to help a sub-group write a report about something that they called *Experience and Application Research*. Strange term yes, but what it means is research and design of ICTs by, with, and for users. It encompasses the social sciences and humanities. It would have enabled DG INFSO to move to a non-linear innovation model. They did not move to a non-linear innovation model!

All they did was, for political reasons (the idea for this came from ISTAG members so not likely that they would do nothing), put the topic into the workprogramme with a small budget and then forgot about it.

Now its 2013, and I am at workshop in Ghent. It is about *Future Internet Research and Experimentation* (FIRE), and someone from DG CONNECT is presenting the research model – it is a linear one. Someone speaks and tells them that this is not the way to develop internet technologies. When the absence of users in DG CONNECT's linear process is mentioned, the immediate response is: "yes we need to involve more users." It seems that no-one in the room understands the point made by the person who challenged this linear model. I do, he was talking about non-linear innovation, in which there is *Experience and Application Research.*

We speak afterwards, exchange business cards, and sympathise with each other – we are among people whom I call Prometheus.

Back in time now to 2006, and that consultation workshop that I mentioned in the previous chapter, for not only were we discussing the *front-end* of design, but also something called *Emotional Content of Design* – hence psychologists were present. Nothing was done about this topic – it never appeared in the workprogramme. It should have for it is exactly what you need if you want to be like Apple and design products that are not technologies but experiences. Back once more to that thing called *User Experience (UX) Design*. Apple has mastered this, and so have other ICT companies, not just in the US but also in Europe.

This too raises interesting questions about the relevance of research funded by the European Commission!

So what purpose DG CONNECT?

Art, ICT and STARTS: DG CONNECT and yet one more story of woe

This is a nursery rhyme:

> *I'll tell you a story*
> *About Jack a Nory;*
> *And now my story's begun;*
> *I'll tell you another*
> *Of DG CONNECT;*
> *And then my story,*
> *Will not be done,*
> *Because later I will,*
> *Tell you another, then another, then ...*

This is a very European Commission story:

STARTS is the current story of woe (probably one of many). What we find is that back in 2012, the European Commission issued a communication addressing the promotion of cultural and creative sectors for growth and jobs in the EU – do not bother looking in the ICT ART CONNECT study report because you will not find reference to it. At about the same time we find DG CONNECT saying that art can be used to make industry more competitive, but offering no evidence for this, but nevertheless it places this failing institution in a position of being able to say that it has taken a lead in addressing what is said in the aforementioned European Commission Communication:

"Horizon 2020 will govern the EU support to research and innovation activities and promote a better exploitation of the industrial potential of policies of innovation, research and technological development. It aims to reinforce competitiveness across a range of emerging industries and sectors, which is of particular relevance for cultural and creative sectors. It will support technological developments in relation to these sectors, such as innovative technologies for the creation and use of creative content and innovative materials for creative industries. Horizon 2020 will also explore new forms of innovation, such as social innovation and creativity, to enhance positive inter-cultural dynamics in Europe and with international partners."

So with ICT Topic 36 planted in the ICT workprogramme, DG CONNECT can make all sorts of claims to boost its image. And when in 2014, Commissioner Designate Oettinger replied to the questions put to him by the European Parliament, he was able to say in response to the question from the Committee on Culture and Education about cultural aspects being taken into account in a horizontal way in all Union policies:

"Artistic creativity and critical thinking are essential for innovation in today's digital world. Already, highly innovative companies thrive on a strong link between artists and their engineers; Daimler has set up a lab exploring futures of urban transport with artists; and eminent art centres like BOZAR engage more and more with technology. The EU's digital funding programmes help support such multidisciplinary teams. In the H2020 programme we are supporting Arts for ICT with €6 million over 2016-17. We are also encouraging our EU-funded ICT projects to spend 1% of their budgets on links with the Arts."

Nice for those concerned, only there is no evidence to support what DG CONNECT has turned STARTS into.

Interestingly, Oettinger was also asked how he would ensure that the cultural and creative sectors are not subordinate to economic interests solely. He did not provide an answer to this question. This is because they will be subordinated to economic interests, so we are back once more to the matter of the *lack of learning from past experiences and programmes.*

Back in 1999 there was a European Commission funded Coordination and Support Action (CSA), funded by a DG CONNECT predecessor, that undertook a study to discover the research activities that would best help the development of European Electronic Games industry. The reason for the study was that: the electronic games industry was not taken seriously by the European Commission because it involved the use of embedded microprocessors for leisure activities – play! The study was a belated attempt to address this myopic view.

Should we mention ICT Topic 35? Why not since we are exposing the true nature of DG CONNECT!

ICT Topic 35: Enabling responsible ICT related research and innovation. Under this topic one finds these words:

"From this wide range of issues, proposals are expected to focus on one or both of the following clusters:

- How can we avoid the traps of ICTs ending up in isolating humans behind their screen, or harnessing them in a passive role? In the forthcoming hyperconnected era, it is essential to acknowledge the dual human aspirations for relationships and for freedom, and the dynamic nature of the relationships between humans and artefacts.

- What are the conditions for ICT-enabled innovations to generate interesting and rewarding jobs, and reduce the risk of excluding sections of society from the labour market? What economic models can ensure a fair sharing of the created added value?

Social scientists already know the answers to these questions, and have known them since way back in the twentieth century. In the 1980s there was extensive research undertaken that deals exactly with these questions. Unfortunately it looks very much like the answers provided by social scientists do not fit with technologists' strange ideologies.

But no matter! The whole exercise is just a political one, so that DG CONNECT can say that it is addressing these very important issues. But its predecessor DGs did exactly the same in the late 80s and early 90s. This is the true nature of DG CONNECT. So what purpose DG CONNECT?

Art, ICT and STARTS: DG CONNECT Theatre and that statement "... not a single scientist, engineer or designer could ever think of ..."

So now we return to the matter we wrote about several chapters past, when we addressed DG CONNECT's theatre, namely the ICT 2015 conference session that went by the name *Driving Innovation through Creativity and the Arts*. Watching from a far we observed one speaker saying, like many who have attached themselves to DG CONNECT and STARTS, yet another ridiculous thing: "... artists working on new technology for dance theatre, when brought into the brainstorming, came up with an idea that not a single scientist, engineer or designer could ever think of – projecting a virtual follow-me car on the windscreen and the driver just follows this virtual car ..."

Now we could at this point begin to write about visual thinking, and the long tradition in engineering of visual thinking along with the development of design tools that enable and support this visual thinking. And no, we are not talking about data visualisation, although that is certainly part of the issue. Perhaps here too we could write about the (not too well understood) damage that the digital computer has had upon this visual design tradition. Perhaps too we could write about the theories from cognitive science and macro economics that shed further light on why people like engineers (and artists) seem to become focused on certain realisations of technology, and perhaps we could shed even more light on matters by writing about design theory.

"Hey! You're being too theoretical!"

"Yes indeed, for theory, as one day you will discover, when it's far too late, is everything. Bad luck!"

That was us, Julia and Paul, responding to the notional person from DG CONNECT.

The statement made by the speaker at the DG CONNECT theatre event, was just a vested interest speaking to people who are either ignorant of what is being discussed or do not care because there is a fool with public money to throw away, and we all know that fools and their money are soon parted.

So in response to the statement: "… artists working on new technology for dance theatre, when brought into the brainstorming, came up with an idea that not a single scientist, engineer or designer could ever think of – projecting a virtual follow-me car on the windscreen and the driver just follows this virtual car …" we say: that it is not true that not a single scientist, engineer or designer could ever think of such a thing.

There is a classic design example created by someone from the world of STEM who was a visual thinker. He was an electrical engineering draughtsman. His job was to create electric circuit schematics for the London Underground, which is full of electric circuits. Circuit schematics are a visual tool; they are not full presentations of the complexity of the routing of and location of cables and electrical equipment:

schematics are simplified symbolic representations, and, if one were inclined to theory, which we are, there is a connection here between the world of STEM and the world of the arts, but we are not going to explore here that matter, because we are obviously far too theoretical for DG CONNECT. What we note is that, this engineering person, produced something that no artist could ever think of, the London Underground map, which is just a electric circuit schematic applied to the problem of helping travellers on the London Underground navigate around the network. We are of course being facetious. But, without a background in electrical engineering, could an artist have produced this design? The year was 1931 and the draughtsman's name was Harry Beck. The map was trialled with the public in 1933 and was an instance success.

Is there another example? Why of course there is. The person is Steve Jobs and the company is Apple Computers. He did not invent the graphical user interface for the Personal Computer. He took it from Xerox PARC, who it would seem got the idea from somewhere else. The result was the Apple Macintosh. Now graphical user interfaces are the norm.

The point is that people in the world of STEM, can and do think in visual terms, and the results are there for people to see – those people that is, who want to see. We will not bore you with all the details of the visual design tools that have been developed by engineers over the years. No artists involved!

So, Steve Jobs and Apple ...

Art, ICT and STARTS: DG CONNECT ignorance – Steve Jobs, Apple and the liberal arts

There is a picture on the internet of Steve Jobs, at the launch of the Apple iPad in 2010, standing next to a road crossing sign with one sign pointing to technology, and another pointing to liberal arts. This is being used in DG CONNECT's presentations – did Steve Jobs advocate the use of artists in Apple research and product development? The picture suggests that this is the case, so it seems like he did! Or did he?

I wonder if anyone in DG CONNECT knows what constitutes the liberal arts, and what the term means, or if they know what Steve Jobs was referring to? Not that it matters if one is desperately trying to find evidence in support of what you decided, long ago, to do.

Now we list some of the liberal arts: languages; literature; linguistics; mathematics; biology, chemistry, astronomy, earth sciences; philosophy; religious studies; economics, sociology, history ...

We look forward to the new prizes that DG CONNECT will be offering to those who work at the nexus of science, technology and philosophy, at the nexus of science, technology, and psychology, at the nexus ... I think we will be waiting a long time!

So, to the matter of defining the liberal arts: The liberal arts are those subjects or skills that in classical antiquity were considered essential for a free person to know to take an active part in civic life, included participating in public debate.

So Steve, want to say something?

"The reason that Apple is able to create products like iPad is because we try to be at the intersection of technology and liberal arts, to be able to get the best of both. I think our major contribution [to computing] was in bringing a liberal arts point of view to the use of computers."

And now we travel back in time to 1996, when Steve Jobs, at that time still at Nexus, was interviewed by Fresh Air's Terry Gross:

"In my perspective ... science and computer science is a liberal art, it's something everyone should know how to use, at least, and harness in their life. It's not something that should be relegated to five percent of the population over in the corner. It's something that everybody should be exposed to and everyone should have mastery of to some extent, and that's how we viewed computation and these computation devices."

What he was referring to was Apple's embracing of the graphical user interface and mouse, which is something that Microsoft did not understand, and consequently did not embrace till about ten years after Apple – they sound like DG CONNECT, with the proviso that is does not take DG CONNECT ten years to catch on, but about 25 years!

And if you want to embrace design of products that are beyond the technocentric, you need more than technologists –

you need sociologists, anthropologists, psychologists, ethnologists, and designers who understand modern design practices and the difference between *front-end* design and *back-end* design. See, we did not mention artists! Do you want to include one? Go ahead, but there is no need to sing and dance about it. But as we have said before, including an artist in a design team, for example to undertake design sketching in the sense that Buxton uses the term, is not necessarily the same thing as using art. Then to this mix add all the other people that are needed – from marketing, engineering, manufacturing, research and development, sales, business management, etc.

The ICT sector beyond Apple also does this, but DG CONNECT is not part of the ICT sector so it would not know about this, being as it is, caught-up in the past. It is however, easy enough to find out find about these modern design practices – just buy a 20 euro book, or speak to people who know about modern design practices in ICT – once again that eliminates DG CONNECT.

And when one looks closely at STARTS, one is left asking a rather important question: where is the ICT sector, the core constituency of DG CONNECT, in this STARTS Platform? Are ICT companies such laggards that they have nothing to contribute, or is it the case that, having been over this ground over 15 years ago, they look upon DG CONNECT as the laggards? Here is a comment about DG CONNECT's STARTS initiative from someone in the ICT sector who works in product development:

"It is a lot of nonsense. Companies working in ICT have already developed the processes that address what DG CONNECT is talking about."

I am sure that you will find some laggards in the ICT sector, and there is no doubt that processes can be improved, but if you do not understand the state-of-the-art, or the challenges, you will only produce what you have produced – that very technocratic construction known as STARTS.

So DG CONNECT keep grasping desperately for evidence. But evidence of these so-called spill-overs you will eventually discover, is hard to find. All you will end up doing, is stating with *conviction*, that science, technology and the arts can foster innovation, which we note is what, in the END, you have been reduced to doing, having found no evidence. And then you will just engage in make-believe.

You can fool all the people some of the time, and some of the people all of the time, but you cannot fool all of the people all of the time.

Here is a paraphrasing of an old, alchemists' (artists') saying:

> *DG CONNECT seekest hard and findest not;*
> *We seek not and find.*

And keep saying ridiculous things for we so love your words, which brings us nicely to the next chapter – for we have saved the best (worst) for last!

Art, ICT and STARTS: DG CONNECT and the saying of ridiculous things

Before the STARTS circus is done, many will have said ridiculous things that they will regret as they engage in singing and dancing to the puppeteers score, and a very good example of the saying of stupid things can be found in the recording of DG CONNECT's SSH RRI information day (See Appendix: web link #8). It is a long recording, being a whole day, but the snippet you need, the presentation of ICT topic 36, is only 10 minutes in duration, and can be found at about six hours and 50 minutes in, just after the presentation for topic ICT 28. And as for the presentation slides, these are available online (See Appendix: web link #9).

So, according to DG CONNECT, art is a hammer! The quote is from Bertolt Brecht, "Art is not a mirror held up to reality but a hammer with which to shape it." Or is it? This is a contested quote for it is also recorded that Brecht may have actually said: "As an artist – and remember that you are one – what daily hammer blows carrying your signature are helping to shape reality?" Not the same thing!

And in the case of STARTS, it is not so much a matter of art shaping reality, but DG CONNECT shaping a reality that suits them – creating the myth, the delusion that they are in someway hip cool – "hey look as us they say, aren't we the cleaver ones!" No you are not – you are ignorant technocrats – why so smart yet so stupid?

Art is many things, for there is a theory that art is that which reflects the life of the community and the life of the community includes everything, such as people constructing for themselves images, as DG CONNECT are doing, and art can also be the hammer that is used to smash this self-constructed image. So to the matter of smashing DG CONNECT's self constructed image.

"Roughly speaking the idea of STARTS is to bring together something that was split I would say in the twentieth century, that is technology and design, which are more solution oriented, and bring it together again with the arts and sciences which are more question oriented." Thus says this European Commission DG CONNECT official!

Am I the only person in the real world who recognises that this Commission official is talking what the Americans (bless them) would call bullshit? The circus has indeed come to town, and is full of people who want to be clowns!

Someone evidently needs to study sociology, for Max Weber was writing about separation, or division of labour and specialisation as it is known, in the nineteenth century (the legal-rational model of bureaucracy). Indeed you will find the matter dealt with much earlier in, for example, the writings of Adam Smith in The Wealth of Nations (1776) and Andrew Ure in The Philosophy of the Manufacturers (1835). Frederick Winslow Taylor (1856-1915) is another (infamous) name linked to obsessions with division of labour and specialisation, as is Henry Ford.

Best not to talk about Descartes and his fragmentation recipe, but he certainly set the scene for the fragmented and reductive mind.

This inclination towards separation though, in the modern world, is largely an Enlightenment thing! This is also why you are so obsessed with this magical word – creativity. But separation can be found earlier. Let us now go back in time to Ancient Greece and lo and behold what do we find Socrates saying, but "One man cannot practice many arts with success." And let us not stop there, for look into history, in the history of Ancient Egypt, and one finds bureaucratic organisation of the State and – specialisation. When civilisation developed, so did specialisation and the disciplinary Tower of Babel came into being.

Europeans are very much still by nature, Ancient Greeks, and Romans too, but have not understood that it will be Buddha, Confucius and Lao-tze that will determine the future of humanity. The *Vainglorious Enlightened Ones* are in serious trouble!

So, the Europeans have dug for themselves these deep pits of specialised ignorance, for reasons that they have long forgotten, and then from within them, they speak of that which they are no longer able to understand. Oh the delights of the reductive and fragmented mind!

And as for design being "more solution-oriented", I think that I should point out that, those who graduate in the subject called design often do so from Art and Design schools, with degrees in? Guess what!

Anyone who has studied design, or knows anything about it, will know that design is about asking questions and experimentation. The good designer always challenges the design brief, which is what those who undertook the, now infamous, ICT ART CONNECT Study should have done, for they evidently did not study the right things. Technologists are also oriented to asking questions and experimentation, otherwise there would be no solutions!

And as for scientists been oriented to asking questions, one only has to look at medical science to realise that both understanding and solutions are being pursued, so it is not just a *question of questions*. Engineering, technology and science are complex areas covering a vast array of activities and to reduce these to some convenient labelling is … an act of the reductive and fragmented mind.

Reality: this categorisation of people as being more solution-oriented or more question-oriented is just a convenient classification used by DG CONNECT because they have no sound understanding of why artists should be involved with the ICT Programme. Neither do they have a sound strategy.

As for the differences – and let us be clear here that there are many – between they who come from art and design, and they whom are often referred to as STEM people: to those that come to know and understand and who can also transcend, does the future belong, while the rest, such as DG CONNECT, will to the past be condemned.

And we learn that STARTS is to be rolled out across the whole of Horizon 2020. Government and Research Funding Agency officials in Washington DC, Tokyo, Beijing, New Deli, and other places, must be rolling on the floor with laughter.

Who needs enemies when you have friends like DG CONNECT?

Directors General in other research DGs, and officials in the Member State administrations, is it not time to put a stop this nonsense and to go back to the drawing board (the design pun is intentional) and to start asking questions about how the arts and design, and other disciplines not traditionally linked to ICT research, can be used in research, development and innovation? The starting point for this is clearly to remove DG CONNECT from this process and involve external people (clearly not those whose are now involved in STARTS) who do know something, and just say to them the honest thing – we, the European Commission, no nothing about this topic, so please begin to explain, on the understanding that we will be undertaking *due diligence* processes about what you are saying and advising.

This of course raises the issue of what types of art practices to be involved with – words like expanded fields of practice, socially engaged art, discourse, and critique, immediately come to mind. We offer no further advice, but at least now you know that there are different types of arts practice, and some, especially those engaged in *jumping around with celebratory glee about STEM*, and whose sole purpose is to extract money from the European Commission (and others foolish enough to listen to their ideology), are not the ones that you should be talking to.

The ideological statement that all H2020 projects should have an artist in residence is just what it is – an ideological statement made by vested interests. A strategic approach is what you need. Artists are not special people, endowed with privileged knowledge, and to think that they are is to just reproduce the elitist power structures and processes that are now self-evidently shown to be failing.

"What's that I hear? Is someone speaking? I'm afraid that you will need to speak-up for your voice is very faint, speaking as you are from a far distant time and place – known as the past. Oh, I see, you're saying 'he's too theoretical'."

Want to watch some more nonsense? See the presentation at the beginning of the SSH information day (See Appendix: web link #8) on ICT Topic 35, the sister area to ICT Topic 36. This official is talking about doing once more, that which was done in the 1980s: Howard Rosenbrock in the UK, Pele Ehn in Sweden, Andrew Ainger at BICC Technologies.

Welcome, DG CONNECT to the past …

Art, ICT and STARTS: DG CONNECT Ends

"Several efforts around the world are under way now to integrate art and technology development. For example, the Interactive Institute in Sweden has five national art and theatre schools linked with research institutes. Similarly the European Commission's i3 initiative has tried to forge links. The US is behind in all this. The motivation is economic – Europe feels like they are behind the US and Japan in technological innovation and are desperate to catch up – even to the extent of including artists."

That was Stephen Wilson, Director of the Conceptual Information Arts Program at San Francisco State University, speaking in 2000. He was of course referring to, in effect, DG CONNECT, which is why we should most certainly be asking: what purpose DG CONNECT?

Now, here in 2016, once again, and most probably in ignorance of their previous involvement with artists, DG CONNECT is even more desperate than they were in 2000. And as they reach out in desperation to artists for a second time, not only are they still seeking to catch up with the US and Japan, but are doing so terrified that China will eclipse Europe in economic terms. This of course China will do, and when the history of this epoch changing event is written, one of the chief architects of Europe's economic downfall will be identified as the European Commission's DG CONNECT.

Now it is time for the curtain to fall. The performance is over, and we take what we have learned and apply it elsewhere, far away from DG CONNECT. But as Julia takes her bow, she has one more surprise, for, here at the END, she has invited Charles Dickens to comment upon DG CONNECT's STARTS initiative:

"I look, I see, I observe, and once more that unpleasant character Ebenezer Scrooge takes shape in my imagination, and noting that his spectra increasingly haunts the modern world, with its fixation on money, and its abandonment of those who are insufficiently able to operate in the efficient way that your economic system demands, being as it is, infatuated with efficiency, and all that implies in terms of human suffering, I speak only one, very distinctive word to DG CONNECT: humbug."

Julia has also invited William Shakespeare to speak a few summary words about the content of this book:

"If this be error and upon me prov'd, I never writ, nor no man ever lov'd."

Thus as the stage lights begin to dim, Julia in one closing act, steps forward, and standing in the single spotlight that remains lit, visible to all, yet at the same time, invisible, she speaks these concluding words:

"What is STARTS? It is but a tale of the wrong people, looking in the wrong places, for the wrong things, and for the wrong reasons."

ENDS

Appendix

Active versions of the following web links can be found at:
www.cheshirehenbury.com/science-technology-and-the-arts

Web links mentioned in the text:

#1

www.cheshirehenbury.com/moments-in-time/preliminary-exegesis.html

#2

manifesto.humanities.ucla.edu/2009/05/29/the-digital-humanities-manifesto-20/

#3

www.cheshirehenbury.com/ict-art-connect

#4

paultkidd.blogspot.co.uk/2016/05/when-distinguished-professor-of-art-and.html

#5

www.youtube.com/watch?v=zYl_3qGXuRE&feature=youtu.be

#6

www.cheshirehenbury.com/paulthomaskidd/paultkidd-this-is-not-art.html

#7

www.cheshirehenbury.com/paulthomaskidd/paultkidd-artist's-creativity-elixir.html

#8

https://scic.ec.europa.eu/streaming/info-day-on-rri

#9

www.cheshirehenbury.com/ict-art-connect/ict-art-pdf-files/STARTS%20Presentation-SSH%20RRI%20Info%20Day.pdf

#10

A short 10 minute clip of the relevant part of the recording available at #8, can be found at:

www.youtube.com/watch?v=EOD7IkeBjtY

www.ingramcontent.com/pod-product-compliance
Lightning Source LLC
Chambersburg PA
CBHW060442040426
42331CB00043B/1087